James H. Wood
photograph taken 1910

"STONEWALL" JACKSON

His Campaigns and Battles

And "The Regiment" As I Saw Them

by
James H. Wood
Captain, Co. "D"
37th Va. Infantry Regiment

With an Appendix
by James Power Smith
Aide-de-camp of Lt.-Gen. T.J. Jackson

THE CONFEDERATE
REPRINT COMPANY
☆　　☆　　☆　　☆
WWW.CONFEDERATEREPRINT.COM

Stonewall Jackson
His Campaigns and Battles
by James H. Wood

Originally Published in 1910
by The Eddy Press Corporation
Cumberland, Maryland

Reprint Edition © 2016
The Confederate Reprint Company
Post Office Box 2027
Toccoa, Georgia 30577
www.confederatereprint.com

Cover and Interior Design by
Magnolia Graphic Design
www.magnoliagrapicdesign.com

ISBN-13: 978-0970852595
ISBN-10: 0970852592

Affectionately dedicated to my two sons and two daughters, J. Harvey Wood, Jr., William Scott Wood, Gertrude Wood Dillard and Mary Wood Harris – the only living members of my family.

The Virginia Military Institute

CONTENTS

☆ ☆ ☆ ☆

PREFACE

☆ ☆ ☆ ☆

These brief memoirs of the War between the States have been written with care. More elaborate detail might have been employed but habits of a professional life have led to terseness of expression. Hence the story unembellished is given, based on personal recollections aided by facts from others and such records as I have been able to reach, including *Strickler's Statistics* of dates of battles.

No effort has been made to do more than to give a brief account of the events seen and known directly or from sources above mentioned. This was undertaken for the purpose of leaving to comrades who still live, to the families of those who are dead, to our own families and to posterity some record, from our view-point, of the most stirring events and enactments of our lives.

To the extent of my rank I was a participant in the scenes described – except two battles – from which disability from wounds prevented. "The Regiment" creditably participated in all.

The performance of this work, though unavoidably deferred, is a duty I have long since felt
incumbent upon myself as well as others who can and
care to do so, to give to our country the benefit of our
testimony as we saw it, of the achievements, sufferings
and sacrifices through which our comrades and
country passed in those eventful years before the same
shall fade from our memory. Our ranks are rapidly
thinning and soon there will be none left to tell the
tale; hence the importance of the testimony of actors
who yet live. From their direct testimony truth can be
reached by the future historian. It is becoming in us
and we do revere the memory of our dead comrades,
thousands of whom sleep in unknown graves, and
their achievements and devotion to the cause they
believed to be just have almost been forgotten. Yet
while the questions involved in the War were forever
settled and so accepted in good faith by the people
of the South, it is the duty of the survivors to preserve
from oblivion the names and deeds of their dead
comrades. To this end this narrative, for whatever it
is worth, has been written.

> But words are things, and a small drop of ink,
>   Falling like dew upon a thought, produces
> That which makes thousands, perhaps mil-
>   lions, think;
>   'Tis strange, the shortest letter which man
>   uses,
> Instead of speech may form a lasting link
>   Of ages; to what straits old Time reduces
> Frail man, when paper – even a rag like this,

Survives himself, his tomb, and all that's
    his.

                    – Lord Byron.

    I have not mentioned many interesting events, including skirmishes and picket fights – many of which developed into small battles. Nor have I mentioned the hard marches through snow, ice, water, mud and rain, many almost shoeless, poorly clad, hungry, shivering with cold, worn, exhausted, sleeping upon the cold and wet ground, ill and suffering – because memory dimmed by years would not permit the attempt. As it is I cannot hope to have avoided mistakes. After the lapse of so much time it would hardly be possible that some misconception or misunderstanding of an event or events should not occur. In such case I would be glad if apprised of it, to make such corrections as I may be able.

    I regret not being able to procure photographs of the others of the Field and Staff Officers and of not being able to procure a roster of the Junior Officers and men of the regiment for insertion in these pages, but as it is I send this volume forth for such consideration as it may receive.

                    James H. Wood.
                Of Bristol, Virginia.
           New York, May 2, 1910.

Gen. Robert E. Lee

CHAPTER ONE

☆   ☆   ☆   ☆

Virginia Military Institute. The Flag Raising. Growing War Spirit.

The growing discontent and excitement in 1860 and the early part of 1861 will ever be remembered by those who passed through that period. At and before this time I, then in my teens, was a cadet at the Virginia Military Institute located at Lexington, Virginia.

For some years prior to this, the questions of political difference between the sections of the United States designated as North and South had been discussed in Congress and on the hustings with increasing acrimony and divergence. The two great political parties, Democrat and Whig, had long been contestants for political supremacy, but in 1860 the Republican party, theretofore greatly inferior in numbers and strength to either of the others, elected Abraham Lincoln sixteenth President of the United States. This was attributed to a division in the Democratic party and the nomination of candidates by each of its two factions. This triumph of the Republican party increased anxiety and apprehension in the people of the South as to their institutions and rights.

Then followed the assembling of the National Congress on the first Monday in December; the secession of South Carolina, December 20th 1860; of Alabama, January 11th, 1861; of Georgia, January 19th; Louisiana, January 26th; Texas, February 1st; the evacuation of Fort Sumter by the Federals, April 14th; the call by Lincoln for troops to coerce the seceded States, April 15th, the secession of Virginia, April 17th; of Arkansas, May 6th; of North Carolina, May 20th; of Tennessee, June 24th; and by acts of the Provisional Congress Missouri was admitted as a member of the Confederate States of America, August 20th; and Kentucky on December 10th, – and of these States the new nation was organized.

Leaders in the field and not on the forum were now being considered and looked to. Sons of the South who had been trained at West Point and a long list of trained soldiers from the Virginia Military Institute, as well as its professors, educated and trained in the science of war, were justly of first consideration. Many of these and many laymen, as well as many members of the then corps of cadets, won enviable distinction in the four ensuing years. The V.M.I., the West Point of the South, now disclosed its inestimable worth to the new nation born at Montgomery, February 18th, 1861. It may be of interest to relate here an incident which disclosed in advance a military chieftain of whom but little was known until the opportunity came for him to discover his merit. Men before this period who had filled mediocre places, began to burst forth in new light as opportunity came. An incident of one, then a quiet V.M.I. professor, now known to history and the world, is worth preserving. It occurred in March, 1861, at Lexington.

The secession of Virginia had not then occurred, but the step was being hotly contested on the hustings between opposing parties. The corps of cadets was almost unanimous for, and the county of Rockbridge and the town of Lexington at the time overwhelmingly against, secession.

Lexington was the home of honest John Letcher, then Governor of the State, whose potent influence was understood to have thus molded public sentiment. The secessionists were enthusiastic and intolerant; the unionists sedate and determined. The war spirit had grown rapidly and had spread to all classes. Members of the corps were almost daily hoisting on barracks secession flags which were promptly taken down by order of the Institute authorities, such evidences of sentiment thus displayed on a State Institution not being permissible while the State was yet a member of the Union. At this time a fine volunteer company composed of young men of Lexington and vicinity, with Capt. Sam Letcher, brother of the Governor, at its head, was being regularly drilled on Saturdays of each week.

The war spirit had now grown so intense that but a spark was needed to set its smouldering fires into a consuming flame. To emphasize their sentiments, the opposing parties without concert or understanding, conceived the plan of raising flags; one the Stars and Bars, the other the Stars and Stripes. The following Saturday was chosen as the day. Due advertisement had been given by both parties. This brought large numbers of people to town, most of whom came provided with such arms as the husbandman of that day had. The number of unionists was more than four times greater than the number of secessionists. The latter soon ran up their flag in the court house yard, addresses followed and the small crowd, including the corps of cadets, was about to disperse to their homes, and the corps to barracks, when the unionists began raising their flag pole some distance up and in the middle of Main Street. From some defect the pole broke and fell, at which the corps vociferously gave vent to expressions of joy, and later returned to barracks more than half a mile away, leaving, however, some three or four of its number behind.

On reaching barracks dinner roll call and the march to and from dinner followed. As ranks were broken on our return from dinner, one of our number who had remained uptown came in breathless haste and announced that House Mountain men had fallen on some of the cadets uptown and killed them. House Mountain is situate some ten or a dozen miles from Lexington, and at and in the vicinity of its base were homes of a good class of people. They were understood at that time to be extremely pro-Union. This information thus given was the needed match to set in flame the pent-up feeling for war. Without a word every member of the corps rushed to his room, seized his musket, cartridge box, bayonet and scabbard and accoutered himself as he ran down the stoops to the front of barracks, thence down the near way to the foot of Main Street near the Letcher residence. Colonel (afterwards General) Smith, superintendent and ranking officer of the Institute, intercepted and tried to turn us back, but his efforts were in vain. On we sped until we reached Main Street. Here Cadet Captain Galloway called out, "Form battalion." This we proceeded to do. All had loaded their muskets and fixed bayonets as they proceeded hither.

While battalion was forming, Major John McCausland (then a sub-professor and afterwards a brilliant Confederate brigadier-general) appeared in front of the battalion and said, "Young men, form and I will lead you up." Col. Smith had now arrived and began to urge our return to barracks. R. McCulloch, of the corps, called to McCausland to lead us on. He replied that his superior officer (Colonel Smith) was in command. Meanwhile the unionists who had realized the situation were but a short distance up the street, preparing for the shock of battle which seemed so imminent. The entreaties to return to barracks and the formation into battalion went on. There stood one hundred and eighty manly youths, armed and equipped and eager for the fray, awaiting the command forward. They were of the very flower of the South. A little later on many of them won marked distinction, boys as they were in armies the soldiers of which for gallantry and endurance have never been excelled in the history of the world.

At this time, Mr. Massey who had won our confidence in his remarks at the flag raising earlier in the day and Maj. R.E. Colston, a professor in the V.M.I. and afterwards a gallant Confederate brigadier-general, galloped up and joined in the appeal for our return to barracks. Meanwhile a greater than any arrived, tall, sinewy, well-formed, a slight stoop in the shoulders, large feet and hands, retreating forehead, blue-grey eyes, straight nose, strong mouth and chin held well to the front, in measured gait, Major Thomas Jonathan Jackson walked up and down before the battalion which he viewed closely, then looked at the surroundings and position of the opposing forces. He uttered no word, but his movements grew more animated each moment, his stature straightened and grew taller and bigger, and his merit was apparent to all and made him the central figure.

Still the formation of battalion went on. A leader who would take command was only needed, while but two or three hundred yards up the street the volunteer company of a hundred young men, well-officered, armed and equipped, were drawn up across the street in battle array, supported by five times their number of the citizens of the town and county, armed with shotguns, rifles and pistols. This warlike scene which had been gathering like a storm cloud during the morning had alarmed the peace-loving citizens and hence an impromptu delegation came forth to intercede for peace and prevent a bloody tragedy which seemed about to occur. These intercessions prevailed, and the corps broke ranks and returned to barracks, discharging their loaded guns as they went.

As soon as we reached barracks, we were summoned by the familiar drum beat to Colonel Smith's section room where we found Colonels Smith and Preston and Mr. Massey on, and Major Jackson near to, but off the rostrum. Colonel Smith proceeded at once to excoriate the corps for its insubordinate conduct. Preston, then Massey, responded pacifically to our call. Last but not least, Major Jackson was called. I remember the scene as if enacted but yesterday. True soldier as he was, Jackson hesitated until Colonel Smith, his superior in rank, asked him to speak. At once he mounted the rostrum and faced his audience. His erect figure, flashing eye, energetic expression, short, quick and to the point, disclosed to the commonest mind a leader of merit. He said, "Military men make short speeches, and as for myself I am no hand at speaking anyhow. The time for war has not yet come, but it will come and that soon, and when it does come my advice is to draw the sword and throw away the scabbard." The personality of the speaker, the force of these simple words thus uttered, elicited a response of approval I never heard surpassed, except by the Confederate yell often heard on the battlefield a little later on. This simple speech and manner of Jackson established in the minds of his audience the belief that he was a leader upon whose loyalty and courage we could rely. How strange it was that this quiet professor who had performed his every duty, monotonous in its regularity, should with a bound leap into view and establish in the minds of his audience that he possessed the qualifications of a brilliant and dashing leader. This was a revelation to his friends and acquaintances, and the estimate of him then formed was shown to be correct by after developments.

It was at the V.M.I. that I first came to know its superintendent and professors, including Jackson. Of the corps of cadets there were young men and boys, representing every State of the South and some of the States of the North. The corps was considered to be one of the finest the institution had ever had. Jackson, ever faithful to duty, now manifested great interest in the political conditions of the country and what they portended. He was instructor in artillery tactics, his favorite arm of the service. He now pushed work, giving great attention to the practical part. Drilling, limbering and unlimbering, target practice and the work incident thereto were very trying to boys in their teens in the hot spring sun, but neither heat nor cold had any terrors for Jackson when duty or the accomplishment of a purpose were involved.

CHAPTER TWO

Corps of Cadets Ordered to Richmond.
March to Staunton, Thence by Rail to
Richmond. Wreck in Blue Ridge Tunnel.
Speech of Governor at Richmond.

Some of the States had passed ordinances of secession and others were following in rapid succession, and war between the States was no longer problematical, but a fact. Virginia hesitated, but soon cast her lot with her sister States of the South and became a part of the new nation. Preparation for war was now pushed forward with great energy. Our corps under command of the State had previously been ordered to Richmond, and its members had been assigned to drill and organize for service the raw volunteers then hurrying thither.

On our departure from the V.M.I. we marched to Staunton, about thirty-six miles distant, thence by rail to Richmond. All were delighted and filled with pride on that beautiful spring morning when the corps in fine array with martial tread marched from the front of barracks, down by the mess hall to the pike, thence on toward Staunton. Colonels Smith and Gilliam and Major Jackson were in charge. Baggage and artillery followed. The bridge across North River was passed, and as we ascended the slope on the other side, we took a last lingering look at the fading outlines of barracks, so dear to us. There our laudable boyish ambitions had been aroused, our hopes kindled and our mental and physical manhood developed. There each was independent of the others, yet all were a band of brothers. Each had learned to obey, and hence knew how to command. The march continued and barracks was soon out of sight. About ten miles out, knapsacks became too burdensome, and a farmer's wagon was impressed for service. This relieved us greatly.

Staunton was reached about 10 o'clock on the night of the day we set forth. The corps was fed and lodged for the night in the hotels. Footsore and weary we slept well and arose at early reveille, chipper and bright and ready for the coming duties of the day. One of the first of which was after breakfast to load on flat cars our battery of four pieces of artillery and our equipment. This was new to us and was hard work. This done, we found we would have two or three hours at our disposal before leaving. Many matrons and damsels, as well as men and boys, had already come to the station to give cheer and encouragement to those who were going forth to do battle for their cause. The neat fitting uniforms of the cadets, to say nothing of their good looks and personal merit – for they were a magnificent body of youths were always pleasing. A little later the crowd of ladies, men, boys and girls with waving handkerchiefs, cheers and huzzas bade us good-bye, and on our way to Richmond we sped.

All went well, until we reached the Blue Ridge tunnel on the old Central, now Chesapeake and Ohio, railroad. Here an exciting and somewhat perilous catastrophe occurred. The train consisted of passenger cars for the officers and corps and flat cars for the battery and baggage. It was special, and hence had no schedule time. When well in the tunnel, which is nearly a mile long, our engine was derailed. The smoke from it filled the cars and the narrow space around them. We could not go forward, for the engine and force engaged blocked the way; nor could we go back, as we would be in danger of being left, as the engine might be ready for duty any minute and would at once pull out. To add to our peril another train from the direction whence we came was about due as per schedule time, and was liable to collide with ours, in which event results could but be imagined. Thus we were held veritable prisoners for nearly two hours, imperiled by the dangers of an oncoming train and the suffocating smoke from our own engine, – our first lesson in the privations and hardships of war. In all this the boys were bright and cheerful. Many witty and some sage remarks were made. Soon, however, we were on our way. Nothing of interest transpired on the rest of our journey, except greetings given us at the stations by the already aroused people who assembled to cheer us on, and the timid requests of the fair maidens for souvenir buttons from our uniforms. Such requests could not be refused. So far was it carried that some of our uniforms were quite disfigured before we reached our destination.

Late in the afternoon Richmond loomed up to view. This was another new sight, for most of us were from rural districts and had never seen a city. From the station we marched to the front of the Capitol building in Capitol Square. Here the corps was reviewed by his excellency the Governor who made a little talk and the compliments paid us were pleasing to boys as we were. He said among other things that war was upon us and much depended upon our work in preparing an army for the field. Then amid the waving of handkerchiefs by the dames and maidens and the huzzas of the men and boys, a large number of whom had gathered to see and greet us, we marched to what was then known as the new fair grounds about two miles west of the city. Here we were quartered in the Exhibition and other buildings. The grounds were beautiful and well suited for a camp of instruction.

Companies and regiments began at once to arrive, undrilled and undisciplined, raw and without arms, except in instances where the individual had given play to his own imagination as to what would be useful in battle, and pursuant thereto had brought the squirrel rifle, the shotgun, the butcher's knife and the pistol, some of the latter of the old pepper box type. A few thought the savage, the dare-devil mein the true indice of the soldier, hence the red hunting shirt, the coon skin cap, the unkempt hair and beard were popular insignia. How ludicrous was it all in the light of after experience! Yet these manifestations were not to be condemned. It is a chapter in their history that ought to give pride to their sons and daughters, because these were the promptings of purest patriotism.

We began early to grapple with the fact that the South was without arms with which to meet a well armed, equipped and powerful foe. These disadvantages to be contended with by the new nation were very great, hence the organization of an army and its equipment as best might be was rushed with great vigor. Enlistment was rapid and troops now entering the camp were anxious to be drilled and instructed. The pulpit, the bench, the bar, the farm, the anvil, the shop and every other calling was represented, ready and willing to take any position from captaincy to private, the latter generally preferred, because of the general feeling of unpreparedness for the responsibilities of office and command, hence there was no unseemly scramble in this respect.

At first the camp was intended for Virginia troops only, but it was soon made the rendezvous of troops of other States as well. This increased the numbers so much that not only the new but the old fair ground was utilized and filled. All added to the excitement, and war and preparation therefore were the absorbing themes of the old and the young, male and female. No male, physically and mentally able to do service, would stay out. Boys of tender years enlisted with the approval of fathers and mothers, and in some instances were even urged to do so. No critical or even cursory examination was applied to the volunteer. Meanwhile the drill, the discipline and the organization went on in a most satisfactory way. The efficient work of the corps of cadets which deserves much praise was soon apparent. It is just to say that the work had been done mainly under the command of our commandant, Col. Wm. Gilliam, Colonel Smith having returned to the Institute and Major Jackson having been commissioned a colonel and ordered to report to Gen. Joseph E. Johnston at Harpers Ferry.

CHAPTER THREE

☆　☆　☆　☆

Richmond Becomes Capital of the
Confederacy. The President.
Presentation of Flag. Ex-President Tyler.
37th Virginia Infantry Regiment

The capital of the new nation had been established at Richmond the latter part of May and later the President and his cabinet removed thereto from Montgomery and entered upon their duties. Anxiety to see the President at our camp, which was now great was soon gratified by an incident then of much interest. A new regiment commanded by Col. Robert E. Withers had arrived at the camp. It was regarded as a fine body of men and its coming created quite a stir of interest in, and respect for it. The ladies of the city desiring to contribute to this respect made with their own hands, as it was then stated, a splendid flag, and requested the President to present it to this regiment. He accepted the honor and on a subsequent afternoon rode on horseback from the city to the camp attended by his cabinet members, officers and aids. This cavalcade attracted universal attention, because the President was its head and all loved and admired Jefferson Davis.

The regiment was drawn up by its proud officers; and other troops and citizens, including many ladies who added grace and beauty to the occasion, assembled nearby. The President stood on a little porch near a small table. The flag was handed him and he held it erect in his right hand, the staff resting on a table, its unfurled folds, rich and beautiful, wafted to the gentle breeze, and it could but be admired. Its makers, however, had not skillfully applied the rules of symmetry and proportion, either in the flag or its staff, for the former was something near the size and shape of a bed quilt and the latter was something less than a bed post. Both were clumsy and disproportionate. The President proceeded with the presentation. His speech was short, but informed, edified and enthused. When he reached the climax among other things he said, "This flag is our symbol of liberty and on behalf of the ladies of the capital of our nation, I give it into hands that will proudly bear it to victory and never let it trail in the dust." Enthused while these and other words were so eloquently uttered, he held aloft, quivering in the air, as if in the grasp of a giant, this heavy and cumbersome flag. The audience had been spellbound until the climax came, and then enthusiasm scarcely had its bounds.

As I remember him, the President was tall, slender, and somewhat cadaverous. I had never before, nor have I since, heard him speak, but on the occasion mentioned I was greatly impressed and shared the general belief in his ability and power.

Other statesmen of the South visited the camp and spoke cheering words to the troops. All were optimistic in their expressed views of the outcome of the war then being entered upon. The most interesting to me of these visitors, however, was John Tyler, tenth President of the United States. He was then full of years, but possessed of much mental and physical vigor. Having learned something of his history, and being but a schoolboy myself just approaching the threshold of life's battles, I was instinctively led to think of him and his life's work, – as a student at William and Mary College, then a fiddler and rollicking youth, as a brilliant lawyer at the Virginia bar, as a captain of a company in the war with Great Britain in 1812, as a brilliant leader in the Virginia legislature, as Governor of the State, as Representative and then Senator in the United States Congress, as successor to the Presidency after the death of William Henry Harrison and his stormy administration. But I have digressed and must return to my intended narrative.

Of the troops now arriving in the camp were the companies of the 37th Virginia Infantry Regiment, to which regiment this narrative will mainly refer. The men composing these companies were young, vigorous and patriotic, but few of them exceeding the age of 35 years. They were from that part of Virginia where milk and honey flow, and were in the main of as good blood as their respective counties contained. One company, with Capt. Shelby M. Gibson at its head, was from the county of Lee; one with Capt. Henry Clinton Wood at its head, from the county of Scott. Three with Capts. John F. McElheney, —— and Simon Hunt at their respective heads, from the county of Russell; and five with Capts. John F. Terry, James L. White, Wm. White, Robert Grant and George Graham at their respective heads, from the county of Washington.

These companies as designated by letter and their successive captains, brought about by casualties and other causes during the ensuing four years of war, were as follows:

Company "A" – Capt. John F. Terry, later Charles Tailor, still later William Lancaster.

Company "B" – Capt. William White, later Benjamin P. Morrison.

Company "C" – Capt. John F. McElheney, later John Duff, still later John P. Fickle.

Company "D" – Capt. Henry Clinton Wood, later James H. Wood.

Company "E" – Capt. Shelby M. Gibson, later Samuel Shumate.

Company "F" – Capt. George Graham.

Company "G" – Capt. —, later — Bussey.

Company "H" – Capt. Robert Grant, later Felix Duff, still later James Berry.

Company "I" – Capt. Simon Hunt, later Thomas Smith.

Company "K" – Capt. James L. White, later John A. Preston.

These captains, as well as their subordinate officers, were men of character and in the main of strong personality. Some of them were educated and trained soldiers. Samuel V. Fulkerson of the county of Washington, who had served in the war with Mexico, a man of ability and high standing, left the circuit bench to lead this regiment as its colonel. Robert P. Carson of the same county and Titus V. Williams of Taswell county, both educated and trained soldiers were in the order named lieutenant-colonel and major. No doubt could exist that such a body of patriots so well officered needed but proper training in systematic cooperative effort to become most efficient soldiers. This work of training in which I had no small part showed its worth in effectiveness on the field of battle later on. Doctors C.C. Henkle and M.M. Butler were later on surgeon and assistant surgeon. They were efficient and faithful in their duties.

This regiment will be hereafter referred to as "The Regiment" to avoid a more lengthy means of designation.

Gen. Thomas Jonathan "Stonewall" Jackson

CHAPTER FOUR

Cheat Mountain Expedition. Ordered to
Jackson at Winchester. Expedition to
Bath and Romney. Battle of Kernstown.
Retreat up the Valley.

Robert E. Lee and Joseph E. Johnston, sons
of Virginia, educated and trained soldiers, already
distinguished in their profession of arms, had resigned from the United States Army and had ten-
dered their services to this new nation. Before Virginia completed the details of her alliance with the
Confederacy, Lee was placed in command of the
Virginia forces, which included the corps of cadets.
In the line of duty occasion brought me to his headquarters to receive from him directions for the
performance of special military duty, and thus I had
opportunity to form my own boyish estimate of him.
I judged his age to be in the fifties and that he was in
the prime of life. His presence and bearing were
above criticism, his manner and conversation kind,

firm, direct and self-confident.

But it is needless to comment further now; his career, his fame, his life and his death are familiar history and need no further mention here. It is, however, deemed appropriate to insert the following graceful tribute to the memory of Lee from the pen of Mr. Henry Tyrrell which appeared in *The New York World* on the nineteenth of January, 1910.

> His sun of life grew grander toward its set-
>   ting;
> It shed a dying splendor on his day,
> Then like a benediction, passed away
>   Through twilight calm, gloomed with no
>   vain regretting.
> A soul serene beyond our strife and fretting,
>   In honor firm but yielding to the sway
> Of kindness ever, he shall with us stay
>   Too fair a memory for the world's forget-
>   ting.
>
> His tomb is here. In graven marble pure,
>   Recumbent sleeps his image. All of fame,
> Glory and love that mortal man may claim,
>   In this white stone and this white name
>   endure,
> 'Neath "Robert Edward Lee" might angels
>   write:
>   "Here lies the last and noblest Christian
>   knight."

Joseph E. Johnston, whom I met and knew later, was an able and accomplished soldier and impressed me as being of the same class with Lee. Albert Sydney Johnston, Beauregard and others, distinguished in their profession of arms, had also resigned from the United States Army and had cast their lots with the South. Soon both sides began with great energy to hurry troops to the front. Lee with a scattered force commanded in what is now West Virginia, Joseph E. Johnston at Harpers Ferry and Beauregard at Manassas. The Federals with the nucleus of the old army drilled and disciplined, armed and equipped, were rapidly assembling large forces at strategic points. The Confederates were equally energetic in assembling opposing forces, but they lacked the nucleus, the general discipline, the arms, the equipment, – all but courage. Big Bethel, the first battle of the War, Manassas, and movements leading up to them, as well as movements at other points, are matters of history and are not to be recounted here.

The first service of "The Regiment" was at Laurel Hill in West Virginia with Brigadier-General Samuel Garland, who was soon compelled by the Federals under McClellan to retire because of his advanced and untenable position. His retreat was hasty, circuitous and trying, lasting from July 7th to the 12th, 1861, during which time skirmishes or small battles occurred, in one of which Garland was killed. After his death the brigade took position on the Parkersburg Pike at Greenbrier River under Brigadier-General Henry R. Jackson. This first was a trying campaign in which a number of casualties occurred and much sickness and suffering ensued.

It was from this position at Greenbrier River that the Cheat Mountain expedition into West Virginia in September, 1861, was made. A Federal force had reached in its advance, the crossing of the Parkersburg Pike of Cheat River, half a dozen miles to the west of our position. Skirmishes occurred between observation parties of cavalry, reinforced at times by infantry from the respective sides as occasion required. These experiences were new to officers and men of both armies, and hence a nervous tension was kept up, as the close proximity of the opposing forces threatened to bring on a general engagement at any of these skirmishes. Jackson's brigade consisted of one Georgia, one Arkansas and two Virginia regiments of infantry, a company of cavalry and a battery of artillery aggregating about 3,000 men. Events and happenings as above indicated had continued for some time and thus stood when the Cheat Mountain expedition was entered upon by the Confederates. It was led by Col. Albert Rusk with his own 3rd Arkansas and 37th Virginia regiments. He was to pass to the rear of the enemy and make attack, while Jackson made demonstration in front. The plan had but little promise of success, because of the superior numbers and fortified position of the Federals.

We broke camp near nightfall of September 10th and moved out with two days' rations. Our course was toward the west down Greenbrier River. We bivouaced about midnight after a hard march of fifteen miles. To this point we had the benefit of a fair country road, but not so the rest of the way. We forded Greenbrier River in the early morning and, wet to the waists, began the long, rugged and trackless ascent of Cheat Mountain. The hardships and perils of this expedition can hardly be described. The rocks, the cliffs, the precipices, the river were obstacles that had to be overcome at whatever cost of suffering or peril. Our descent of the mountain on the other side was quite short. In a channel or trough along the top of the mountain near its summit Cheat River flows to the east, while Greenbrier River at the base of the mountain flows to the west. The high altitude made the water and atmosphere quite cold, even for this season of the year. Our course was down this river with no road or trail save the bed of the stream. Its precipitous and cragged banks necessitating an almost continuous wading down, across and back for many times. Late in the afternoon we reached a point near the enemy, but slept on our arms until morning. A reconnoissance, however, disclosed his impregnable position. Our skirmish line exchanged some shots with the outposts and some casualties occurred, but the number I do not recall.

I was brought to think why it all could not have been avoided; but, then as now, a few men on opposing sides led all the others and war resulted. We rested on our arms that night in close proximity to this stronghold, without food, hungry and chilled to the bone and as uncomfortable as it seemed possible to be. The folly of an assault upon the enemy's fort was seen and known, hence the return march was taken up. This was without incident. Many became ill and a number gave up their lives from the hardships and exposures of this expedition. My own illness extended over many weeks, during part of which time hope for a favorable issue almost fled. It was, however, my good fortune to be taken to a good country home and to be attended by a faithful nurse, which perhaps prevented a different result.

When I was convalescing, but yet weak, a young soldier, delirious from pneumonia, who occupied an adjoining room, came to my bedside during the temporary absence of my nurse and seized a heavy, long necked bottle of brandy and raised it as if intending an assault, and apparently was about to bring it down on the head of his prostrate victim, who expected the blow and its serious results, but could do nothing to ward it off. Fortunately, before delivering the blow this crazed man, being consumed with fever, saw through the window an inviting stream of water that flowed by. Quickly replacing the bottle, with catlike swiftness he passed down the stairway and to the stream, and drank copiously of its waters. He was unable to return and was carried back and early the next morning gave up the struggle and passed into eternity.

In October the regiment was ordered to report to Stonewall Jackson at Winchester, and was assigned to the third brigade of Jackson's division. This brigade was now composed of the 37th and 23rd Virginia, First Georgia and Third Arkansas Regiments. Samuel V. Fulkerson was colonel of the first, William B. Taliaferro (pronounced Tolliver) and after his promotion to the rank of brigadier-general, Alexander Talliaferro of the second, — Ramsey of the third and Albert Ruske of the fourth, above named regiments. Soon after this time the 1st Georgia returned to its home and the said 3rd Arkansas was ordered to Manassas and became a part of Hood's brigade. The Tenth Virginia, commanded by Colonel S. B. Gibbons, about May, 1862, and the 1st and 3rd North Carolina regiments, about August or September of that year, were assigned to the brigade and remained with it after that time. Our brigade commanders were: First, Henry R. Jackson, later William B. Talliaferro, and still later George H. Stuart.

We remained in this brigade and division after that time, and future reference thereto will be "3rd Brigade."

Jackson was now a major-general and had been assigned to the command of the valley district. His force consisted of three brigades (1st, 2d and 3d, Ashby's cavalry and about three batteries of artillery, aggregating approximately 10,000 men). In the latter part of December he made an expedition to Bath and Romney which was without apparent results, and it was regarded by his officers and men as unwise. From this a distrust in his ability as a leader arose. The weather was extreme, rain, sleet, snow and intense cold caused great suffering and the actual illness of many. From this and other causes his army was so much reduced that by early spring his entire force did not exceed 6,000 men, at which time the district under his command was beginning to be threatened from different directions and by different commands, aggregating a total force of about 40,000 men. These conditions to many would have seemed appalling, if not hopeless; but not so to Jackson. Instead it was then that his remarkable strategy and skill began to manifest themselves.

He retired from Winchester, moving slowly up the valley to the vicinity of New Town and from there made a demonstration toward Winchester, now occupied by a Federal force of about 12,000 under the command of General Shields. The forces met on the afternoon of March 23d at Kernstown, three miles south of Winchester and a very severe battle was fought, resulting in many casualties on both sides; but superior numbers forced Jackson to retire about dark still further up the valley. The "Regiment" and "3rd Brigade" took a conspicuous part in this engagement and suffered severely. It was then difficult to understand why Jackson should have risked battle with this superior force. This again brought in question his capacity for leadership of a separate army, and but for his courage, sincerity and willingness to share hardships and dangers with his men he would have been held by them in much lower esteem as a commander.

He was freely discussed and his expedition to Bath and Romney and his giving battle at Kernstown freely condemned, because not even probable beneficial results could have been anticipated as viewed by his critics. But when conditions were understood later on, it was apparent that no mistake had been made by

Jackson in either instance. In truth, it is a question whether these events did not save Richmond from capture. McClellan's army of 100,000 men was pressing Johnston back toward the very gates of the city, yet McClellan was not willing to try conclusions until reinforcements could be had, and there was no other source from which they could be procured than from the armies surrounding and threatening Jackson's district – but withdrawal of reinforcements could not be made until Jackson should be overthrown, and thus the danger of a descent by him on Washington or on the rear of McClellan's army removed. Hence Jackson's evident purpose was to keep these 40,000 men from reinforcing McClellan; how well he accomplished this was abundantly shown. At this distance of time it is difficult to discover a material mistake made by him, – since the Bath and Romney and the Kernstown events have been understood – his career was a success and nothing beats success.

Col. Samuel V. Fulkerson
photograph taken 1860

CHAPTER FIVE

Retired to Swift Run Gap. Ewell's Division
Arrives. Battle at McDowell. Battles at
Front Royal and at Winchester.
Bank's Retreat Across the Potomac.

Shields retired in the late spring of 1862 toward the east side of the Blue Ridge, and Banks
with an army of approximately 20,000 men moved
up the valley to Strasburg, thence on toward
Harrisonburg, Jackson slowly retiring before him.
Almost daily attacks, often growing into small battles, were made on the advancing Federals by the
intrepid Ashby; but Jackson's force was too inade-
quate to risk a general engagement.

He, however, would pause at strategic points
until the enemy would concentrate in his front and
would then retire, leaving the ever vigilant Ashby to
keep up appearances – which he would so successfully do that the enemy would not discover the ruse
for days, and when discovered would be thrown into

a state of excitement, because not knowing when and from what direction a blow might be received. Just below Harrisonburg we left the valley pike and went into camp near Swift Run Gap on the road leading through this gap in the Blue Ridge, a strong position susceptible of being held by a small force against many times its number. Thus the way to Harrisonburg and Staunton was virtually open to the advancing foe, but he did not venture on. Ashby's cavalry was not now available to dispute his advance because of the wide field of operation and observation this command had to cover. This field embraced the immediate front, the Page Valley Front Royal and McDowell; thus Jackson was kept informed of every move of the enemy. Here he was reinforced by Ewell's division, bringing his entire force, including the brigade of General Edward Johnston then near McDowell, to approximately 15,000.

Milroy was now pressing Johnston back toward Staunton and had reached McDowell, thirty miles northwest of that city. Jackson now left Ewell to watch Banks and moved with his own division about 6,000 through Swift Run Gap to the east side of the Blue Ridge. His army thought this to be an abandonment of the valley, and the impression became general that Joseph E. Johnston needed reinforcements to save Richmond and that this was our destination; but when we reached the railroad, instead of going east to Richmond, we went by rail west to Staunton, thence by forced march to McDowell. On the afternoon of May 8th the attack on Milroy, whose army was estimated at 8,000, was opened by Johnston's brigade. The Federals occupied a position on the west and at the base of Shenandoah Mountain. A deep and difficult ravine intervened between this position and a low ridge occupied by the Confederates. The use of artillery was almost impossible, owing to the hills and rugged ground; hence the battle was fought almost entirely with small arms and was different from subsequent battles in this, that there was no bayonet charge, but simply each side from its position kept up an incessant fire and roar of musketry at comparatively close range until the end.

The whole scene is yet vivid in my mind as I saw it. Our brigade was well down the mountain when the battle began and the roar of musketry and shouts of the contending forces came up the mountain side to us as we hurried on. There was a kind of horrible grandeur about it all that allured and inspired some, and struck others with trepidation. There were but few, if any, who would not prefer to escape the perils of battle, but a sense of duty made the man of moral courage a good soldier, however mindful he might be of pending danger or of death itself. It is soldiers of this, and not of the physical courage type, that win battles. We moved on; louder and still fiercer the battle grows. Reinforcements are now entering on the Federal side with battle shouts and huzzas, which are answered in grim defiance by the Confederates. Johnston's brigade alone holds the front for the Confederates. Our brigade has now reached the base of the ridge, where we find Jackson who quickly points our position. Here, too, we found the field hospital, the ground strewn with the wounded, the dead, the dying, and still others came down the ridge from the front, wounded and red with blood, assisted or carried on litters. Surgeons and assistant surgeons are doing all they can to save suffering and life, but the scene is too sickening to pause and consider.

On we go up the Ridge, take our position in line and open fire on the enemy. The battle now rages ten times fiercer than before, men fall on every side, some never to rise, while others are wounded and helped to the rear. The smoke of battle settles upon us so dense and dark that we cannot see happenings around us. Begrimed, drinking and tasting the smoke of battle seemed to increase courage and determination, and thus with defiant war cries the battle goes on for some hours. General Johnston was shot and disabled, Colonel Gibbons of the 10th Virginia fell. Captain Terry and Lieutenant Wilhelm, John Lawson and many others of my own company and regiment whose names I do not now recall were killed or wounded. After a lapse of forty odd years it is impossible to recall names. Notwithstanding the horribleness of this scene there was such a mixture of excitement, intensity of purpose, of danger and exhilaration that it was more fascinating than repulsive.

Nightfall came upon us, yet the battle still went on in unabated fury. At this time a Confederate force that had been making its way on the mountain side through the hills and rugged grounds on our right, descended upon the enemy's left and routed him completely from the field. Then came the jubilation over the victory and of each over his own escape from injury. The next sensation was that of grief for the lost and injured. We now went into bivouac, and the following morning started in pursuit of the Federals who retired in haste to Petersburg, about ninety miles from Staunton. Here Fremont joined Milroy and concentrated his army of approximately 25,000 men to resist our further advance. In this retreat the woods were set on fire by the Federals, causing smoke, darkness and gloom, and hence slower progress in the pursuit as well as suffering from the heat and smoke.

About the middle of May, Banks, with an army now increased to approximately 25,000 men, occupied and had fortified Strasburg against attack from the direction of Staunton, eighty miles to the southwest. Ten miles south of Strasburg is Front Royal. Between Strasburg and Front Royal is the north end of Massanutten Mountain, which extends to the South for a distance of fifty or sixty miles, separating Shenandoah from Page Valley. Winchester, twenty miles north of Front Royal, had also been fortified by the Federals and at this place they had assembled large army stores. Thus Banks and his army stood at Strasburg in fancied security while Fremont was concentrating his army at Petersburg to resist further advance of the Confederates. Aided by the smoke and gloom, Jackson withdrew from Fremont's front, leaving a small cavalry force to keep up appearances, and with unsurpassed celerity swept hrough the passes of Shenandoah Mountain, thence down Bridgewater Valley to Harrisonburg where Ewell's division joined him. Thence he passed down the valley pike towards Strasburg, but turned abruptly to the right at New Market, crossed Massanutten Mountain into Page Valley. At the same rapid gait he swept on to Front Royal and on the 23d of May dispersed the force there, capturing many. So rapid and dashing was his movement that the effort of the Federals to burn the wooden bridge spanning the Shenandoah was only partly successful. The damage was repaired so quickly that pursuit was scarcely checked.

Banks at Strasburg ten miles to the north had found out the peril of his army and had earlier in the day begun a precipitate retreat to Winchester, eighteen miles away. Night ended further pursuit, which, however, was resumed early the following morning, and in the afternoon we reached the valley pike at Middletown and there struck the right flank of the rear of Bank's army. The conflict was short but sanguinary. The enemy fled precipitately, leaving his dead and wounded on the field. A number of prisoners also fell into our hands. Our own loss was small. We now pressed forward, continuing the march during the entire night, becoming so weary and worn that we actually slept as we marched. We reached Winchester at early dawn and again encountered the enemy. Our division occupied the left and Ewell's the right. The attack was begun at once.

In our front we found the enemy well posted

behind a stone fence or wall; their well placed artillery further back and more elevated commanded the open approach to this formidable and well-protected force. Our advance was begun in fine order, without rush or confusion – meanwhile shot and shell played upon us. The greater elevation of the Federals caused them to overshoot, hence we did not suffer greatly. At the order to charge our whole line leaped forward with a terrifying Confederate yell, rushed onto and over the stone wall. The loss of the fleeing enemy was heavy. The simultaneous attack by Ewell on the right caused the entire Federal line to give way and the Confederates swept forward in such force and swiftness, dealing such havoc to the Federals, that they were thrown into confusion, panic and rout, and utterly unable to offer resistance to our onward sweep. The pursuit was continued for some miles until forced from exhaustion to halt. Many prisoners were captured and the artillery, small arms and military stores captured were very large. The volume of this capture gave to Banks the sobriquet of "Jackson's commissary." The following day pursuit was resumed by way of Charlestown to Harpers Ferry. Here the Federals made their escape across the Potomac into Maryland.

Lt. Col. Robert P. Carson
photograph taken 1910

CHAPTER SIX

Return to Strasburg. Retired to Port Republic.
The Angle Near Harrisonburg. Ashby Fell.
Capture of Bridge by Federals. Recapture
by Confederates. Battles of Cross Keys
and of Port Republic.

We then returned by forced march to Winchester – the "3rd Brigade" in the lead. On this strenuous march our strength and endurance were put to a severe test. On the second forenoon of our march, if my memory serves me well, we reached Strasburg, thence to the right, two miles out on the Moorfield road. Here we took position to resist the advance of Fremont who was already nearby. At the same time Haze's brigade was ordered to the left on the Front Royal road to resist the threatened advance of Shields from the direction of Manassas. These two brigades were entrusted with the duty of holding open this gap through which the valley pike passed, against these two armies, numbering approximately

51

25,000 and 12,000 men, until the trains including our immense captures and the army of approximately 10,000 worn Confederates passed through and on up the valley.

The margin of time allowed in the calculation was narrow, but accurate with not a moment to spare. In fact we had scarcely taken position when Fremont's advance came in sight and was surprised to find us in waiting and to meet the fire of our skirmish line, the Federals retired to await further preparation for advance. The rest of the afternoon was occupied in maneuvering and reconnoitering by the Federals, and at nightfall their plans seemed matured for an advance in the early morning. But the delay gave the Confederate trains, including captures of stores, prisoners and arms, time to pass up the valley, then during the night the two brigades returned to the pike and brought up the rear. Thus our army was extricated from its extreme peril of a little while before.

Fremont followed in Jackson's wake, while Shields pushed up the Lu Ray Valley on the east side of the Shenandoah, now swollen out of its banks by recent rains, and hence not fordable and without bridges as high up as Port Republic. The bridges, except at Port Republic, had been burned by our cavalry a few days before by order of Jackson. Now followed by an army superior in numbers, while another army was paralleling his march with evident purpose to intercept or impede his progress and thus force an engagement with this combined and overwhelming force, but not disturbed by this apparent peril, Jackson slowly retired before Fremont to Harrisonburg, and there turned sharply to the left toward Port Republic. At this turn the Federals ("Pennsylvania Buck Tails") made a flank attack in force on our rear guard. Col. Bradley T. Johnston of the Maryland line, supported by Ashby, repulsed this attack, inflicting considerable loss on the enemy. Our own loss in numbers was not great, but among the killed was the redoubtable Ashby, which sad loss was deeply lamented by the entire army. No leader stood higher in the estimation of his comrades or had promise of a brighter future.

Passing on we reached the heights on the north side of the Shenandoah, overlooking Port Republic, located in the fork of the river, and a tributary stream entering it on the south side. On the following morning, June the 8th, being adjutant, I read to the regiment, then on Sunday morning inspection, an order for divine service to be held by the chaplains in their respective regiments. Before inspection had been finished, two or three artillery shots in the direction of the village of Port Republic were heard. At this time, Capt. Henry Clinton Wood, who had gone to the village on a business errand, came in breathless haste and stated to our colonel, Fulkerson, that the enemy were in possession of the bridge. This was a wooden structure spanning the main branch of the Shenandoah River from our side to the village. Without hesitation the regiment was formed and proceeded at double quick time through an intervening wheat field to the bridge. On reaching the top of the ridge we saw a cavalry force with two pieces of artillery in possession of the Port Republic end of the bridge. They used their artillery on us with damaging effect, killing two and wounding others. We soon reached the road leading to the bridge, and when within about a hundred yards of it met Jackson riding rapidly from the direction of the bridge.

I was with my colonel at the head of the regiment and saw and heard what occurred and what was said. Jackson turned his horse and in his characteristic way, said, "Charge right through, Colonel, charge right through." As he spoke he seized and swung his cap about his head, uttering a low cheer, adding, "Colonel, hold this place at all hazards." He then turned his horse and rode swiftly toward Cross Keys, where the battle had already begun. We rushed on, and when near the mouth of the bridge the enemy fired one or both of his pieces that were planted at the other end, but the charges took effect in the sides of the bridge and did no injury to us. We captured the pieces and a number of prisoners and horses. No other troops than "The Regiment," and no other commander than our colonel had any part in the capture of this bridge, artillery and prisoners. It was then said, and I believe from the circumstances it is impossible to question its truth, that Jackson, whose headquarters were in Port Republic, had reached the bridge after the Federals, and by the ruse of commanding a change of position of one of the pieces, and while this order was being obeyed, dashed through and met our regiment. This has been questioned, but the facts above stated would seem to be conclusive except as to the ruse, but, that Jackson reached and passed through the bridge after the Federals had taken it and placed their artillery and used it on our approaching column when we were more than a quarter of a mile away cannot be successfully controverted if circumstantial evidence can be relied upon.

The battle of Cross Keys now became more general and continued during the day. In the afternoon the Federals were pressed back as indicated by the sound which continued to recede and were finally beaten and driven from the field which was occupied by the Confederates. The casualties on both sides were heavy. Nothing of importance occurred during the day at Port Republic, except that a few shells were fired by the advance force of Shields, resulting, however, in but little injury. Shields was in hearing of the battle of Cross Keys, but was unable to give or receive aid to or from Fremont on that or the following day because of the intervening Shenandoah, still swollen out of its banks. There was no bridge save that at Port Republic, which in the emergency was a prize well worth a great effort to obtain. Shields had rushed up the river to attain this prize, and his force was now near the village. doubtless he felt elation at the prospect of seizing this bridge, the only avenue of escape for Jackson, who in such event would have been between the two Federal armies and at their mercy, but "the best laid schemes o' mice and men gang af't agley."

By dawn of Monday the 9th, Jackson had crossed his army from the north to the south side of the Shenandoah, burned the bridge, crossed the swollen south branch and moved on Shields, but two miles below. The attack nearest the river was made by two brigades of Jackson's old division with their accustomed vigor. The opposing force with marked gallantry resisted this attack, and being now reinforced, repulsed the Confederates. Our brigade was hurried to their assistance, but before we reached that part of the field, Jackson himself, as was then said, rode into the thick of the battle and called to his men that the Stonewall brigade never retreats. This rallied them to a renewal of the attack, which was now fortunately aided by Taylor's brigade, which had moved along the mountain side under cover of the timber and undergrowth, gaining the left flank of the Federals and at this propitious moment made a vigorous attack. Thus pressed in front and flank, the Federals gave way and broke into a precipitous rout. Many prisoners were taken and the remaining force pursued by the infantry, until exhaustion put an end to further pursuit by them, but was taken up by the cavalry. When the Federals gave way in retreat, Jackson came riding slowly from the left toward the road. His head was bowed and his right hand, gauntleted, was pointing upward. He was alone and seemed oblivious to all around him and presented the appearance of being in supplication or rendering thanks. A number of guns and a quantity of ammunition were also captured. The Federal loss was much greater than the Confederate, caused largely

largely by the Federals becoming confused and thrown together in compact bodies, on which artillery and small arms did greatest execution.

During the day Fremont's army had pushed forward from Cross Keys to the summit of the ridge, bordering the river on the north, and had planted a number of batteries of artillery commanding the road over which we had advanced. We could plainly see, but were out of range of these guns frowning upon us, and we well knew the impossibility of returning by this route. Earlier in the day, however, Jackson had directed his engineers to construct a road along the side of the Blue Ridge to Browns Gap Road, leading across the Blue Ridge. This was done and before nightfall our army passed over this new road in full view of the Federal army and guns, but out of range, and bivouaced along the mountain side for that and two or three succeeding nights, enjoying a greatly needed rest.

The ensuing quiet of Jackson so mystified the Federals that they returned to the valley and towards Winchester. Jackson then returned his army to the valley and went into camp near Weirs Cave. After a few days a rumor gained currency that an advance down the valley was soon to be made by Jackson. The enemy now began to collect his forces for this expected advance. The rumor was strengthened by the arrival at Staunton of Whiting's division to join Jackson. Thus matters stood at the end of this re-markable campaign of but a little over one month, during which brief time the battles of McDowell, of

Front Royal, of Middletown, of Winchester, the angle at Harrisonburg, of Cross Keys, and of Port Republic had been fought and won, and a distance marched of approximately two hundred miles, and the armies of Fremont and Shields were now remote from facilities of transportation and communication with Washington and McClellan. This campaign alone is sufficient to give Jackson and his army a fame that will live in history. Jackson was now more so than before the idol of his army and of the people of the South. He had become known and now shown out like a star of hope, but he was yet to win greater renown.

CHAPTER SEVEN

On to Richmond. Battles at Gains' Mill and
Cold Harbor. Fulkerson Fell. Battles of White
Oak Swamp, Frazier's Farm, Malvern Hill and
Harrison's Landing. Return to Richmond.

There is no purpose in this narrative to reflect
upon the valor and worth of the Federal soldier or
his leaders. This could not truthfully be done; it was
simply a case of Greek meeting Greek, each being
worthy of his foeman's steel. There was, however,
a stronger incentive to heroism for the Confederate
because he fought for home and on his own soil.
Aside from this, the greater numbers in equal battle
generally won; slight advantage, however, in such
cases usually turned the scale.

By the middle of June, Fremont, having heard
of Jackson's return to the valley, began to gather his
forces to prevent onslaught on detached parts of his
army; but by skillful use of his cavalry and outposts,
Jackson kept him mystified, and hence ignorant of

his movements. The great leader was thus able to withdraw from Fremont's front without his knowledge, and again passed through Browns and Swift Run Gaps to the east of the Blue Ridge, thence on to Richmond, a small force being left in Fremont's front to keep up camp fires to conceal the withdrawal. Our march was continued along the Virginia Central Railroad which conveyed to our destination as many soldiers of the advance column as the cars it could supply would accommodate, then trains would return to meet the marching columns and reload and convey as before. This was continued until the army had been assembled near Ashland by the 26th of June, at which date we left the railroad, moving sharply to the left. Our progress was slow and cautious.

In the afternoon of the 27th we heard heavy firing some distance to our right. This was the advance of Hill by way of Mechanicsville and Beaver Dam, from which positions the Federals were forced back towards Gains Mill and Cold Harbor, toward which place our column was also converging. About three o'clock p.m. Hill again struck the enemy to our right and the battle at once became hot and furious. Our column being at a halt, I rode a little way to the right and viewed from an elevation for a brief space of time a part of this battle, half a mile away. The Confederates by a brilliant charge swept the Federals from the field, but by a counter charge of fresh Federal troops the decimated Confederate ranks were in turn forced back over the same open field, which, however, was quickly recovered by fresh Confederates, leaving the dead and dying of both sides lying on this bloody field, promiscuously intermingled. I rejoined the column now moving forward, which soon again halted. The battle now raged and was rapidly extending to the right.

At this time an incident occurred which is related here to show how indifferent to Fate the veteran of many battles becomes when in the face of battle and probable death, for all now knew we were soon to enter the bloody contest going on. Near me was a lieutenant of the regiment, free and easy and not exacting of respect for his rank, familiarly given the sobriquet, of "Spelling-book." A man of apparent intelligence and standing came from the direction of the battlefield toward us. He was of middle age, in evening dress, and wore the conventional silk hat. His mount was a flea-bitten, gray mare of sleepy gait; and his black trousers were well divorced from the tops of his hose. As this unique figure entered the road through the open fence, "Big" John Duff, a humorous young man of the regiment, said to the lieutenant referred to, "Spelling-book, how are you to-day?" The gentleman, thinking himself addressed and thinking to ward off the intended fun at his expense, promptly replied, "Very well, I thank you, how are you?" This attracted general attention, and the fun began. A fusillade of wit, humor and burlesque was fired at this poor defenseless citizen. "Come down out of that hat," "Jump off and grab a root," "Are you a married man or an Irishman?" "Put sinkers to your britches. Bandage your legs," and much more badinage was so cruelly and mercilessly hurled at this object of ridicule who had almost immediately been silenced that he became livid with mortification and chagrin. In desperation he began urging his mare forward by violently digging her sides with his heels, being without spurs or whip. He succeeded in getting her into a pace along the smooth road between the lines of soldiers, the gait being the proverbial pacing of half a day under the shade of a tree. The fun was increased by the boys whistling, "Pop goes the weazel," in perfect time with the gait of the mare, and was continued along the line as he progressed. Finally in desperation he seized his silk hat and began to beat the gray mare to urge her forward. This frantic effort still further, if possible, increased the hilarity, and finally after covering a good distance, enduring an ordeal worse than battle, he turned to the right, entered the woods and disappeared. How soon was the opposite extreme to follow, blood, misery and death; for in less than half an hour we were in the forefront of battle.

We moved forward rapidly and took position in the second or supporting line and the whole moved forward. The Federals occupied a ridge near Gains' Mill that dominated the approaches from which they used with damaging effect their well-placed artillery. We had passed Lee and Jackson on our way and now swept down the long, gentle slope through shot, shell and minnie balls. Near the base of the ridge we were impeded by a ravine, about six feet wide and as many feet deep. Here we met the withering fire of the enemy, but the line in front and we in turn passed this obstacle, thence up the ridge in the face of a most stubborn and gallant resistance by the Federals, who at last gave way and were swept from the field, leaving their dead and wounded. The sight was ghastly and sickening. Our own loss was not so great. Major Wheat, leader of the famous New Orleans Tigers, mortally wounded on the face of the ridge while advancing, said to his men when he fell, "Bury me where I fall," and immediately expired. His request was complied with. This statement is based on what was then understood to have occurred.

Our lines were halted and adjusted near the summit of the ridge and here night put an end to further pursuit. When quiet came to our ranks I accompanied my colonel (Fulkerson) to our front to view the ground. We reached the top of the ridge, but were unable to see, because of the darkness in the low grounds beyond; but the sky being our background made us conspicuous targets for the retreating Federals, hence frequent shots were fired and the balls passed in close proximity to us. We thought them stray shots, however, until convinced by their continuance that we were the targets.

I had stepped half a dozen paces from the colonel to a splendid battery of artillery the enemy had been compelled to abandon, and was speaking to him of the valuable prize. Meanwhile minnie balls continued to pass in the same close proximity to us. My attention was attracted to the colonel. He had been struck and was slowly turning and sinking. I quickly put my arm about him and assisted him to the ground.

I saw he was seriously hurt and had him borne from the field. He requested me to say to the regiment that he had every confidence that it would do its duty, that he did not want it to be affected because of his condition. At the field hospital, despite every effort of our able surgeons, Henkle and Butler, he died of his wounds the following day. Thus passed a good soldier and valuable man to his country. His death cast a gloom, not only over his regiment, but over all who knew him. Our former lieutenant colonel, Carson, a splendid officer, had, because of complete physical disability reluctantly left the service some time before, and our lieutenant colonel, Titus V. Williams, now became colonel, Capt. John F. Terry, lieutenant colonel, and Capt. Henry Clinton Wood, major; all were brave and efficient officers, in and for whose courage and ability the regiment had confidence and respect. I was now promoted to the captaincy of Company "D," being one of the youngest in the army. To accept this promotion, I resigned the office of adjutant theretofore held by me, and Lieut. James L. White, Jr., an efficient and accomplished officer, succeeded to the position.

After burying our dead on the 29th, pursuit of the enemy was resumed. Our course was down the east side of the Chickahominy through deep, tangled undergrowth, marshes and pine thickets. The heat of a burning sun, deadness of the atmosphere in this wilderness of low ground, an afternoon rainstorm of great intensity which covered the already marshy ground with water, then mud, in consequence, making the trackless way still more difficult than before, then the sun reappearing superheating the humid atmosphere, causing prostrations of many and great discomfort to all. Then added to these troubles, water fit for man or beast was difficult to find, and when found was either bitter or brackish. These made up this day of trials.

That night we crossed at Grapevine Bridge to the south side of the Chickahominy, thence on to White Oak Swamp. Here we found the enemy in strong force on the opposite side with no way of approach, except by the road and bridge over which he had retreated. The bridge, and much of the corduroy road, however, had been destroyed, and we were at a halt in this deep, tangled wilderness. An artillery duel was opened and continued until night.

The next morning a furious battle opened at Frazer's farm on the opposite side of the swamp, and raged with great fury. Our way was still blocked, and hence we were unable to give the needed aid to Longstreet, who, from the sound of battle, was being sorely pressed. The next morning the way was opened; we captured some pieces of artillery and pushed on to the battlefield at Frazier's farm. The enemy now retreated to Malvern Hill and here made a determined stand. This was a most formidable position commanding the open, level ground for a mile in front, and protected by a sluggish and difficult stream on our left. Our command took position on a neighboring ridge on the left where we suffered much from the enemy's artillery which dominated our position, from which, however, we could see the entire field. We saw the charge of D.H. Hill, Huger and Magruder across this open field. The formidable position of the Federals with his hundred pieces of artillery and heavy lines of infantry made such an advance appear as a forlorn hope, but the gallantry displayed was splendid. Shot, shell, grape and cannister poured into these brave troops was horrible to behold. They never flinched nor wavered, but pressed forward until recalled. Many dead and wounded were on the field.

Well posted sharpshooters with guns of longer range than ours were very annoying and damaging. Our men were thus picked off here and there with remarkable regularity. In places of such danger good fortune seemed to follow some and bad fortune others. While shells from the enemy's guns were flying thick and fast about us, occasionally exploding in our ranks with direful effect, four men for relief from the nervous tension by the engagement of their attention in something other than the dangers of shells and minnie balls, sat down to a game of cards. A shell soon passed so close that they moved a few feet away to get out of range. A moment later a shell struck and exploded at the spot thus abandoned, tearing a deep gash in the earth, scattering dirt and debris in all directions. Fate, luck or possibly that instinct that perceives pending danger, saved these men from complete destruction. Then, too, it is said and oft times really seemed to be so, "that fortune favors the brave," and these soldiers were brave. A moment later a minnie ball well spent in its force struck a soldier in the forehead, but did not penetrate the skin. He jestingly remarked that they came near getting him that time, and while thus joking, he fell and expired, concussion caused death.

At the risk of prolixity, I mention another incident as the converse of the above, – that misfortune attends the timid. On moving to position, we passed a soldier sitting behind a black oak tree about four feet in diameter. A shell had passed through the tree and had taken off the top of his skull, then passed into a large pile of rails, exploded and scattered the rails in all directions. No one could have imagined danger when thus protected. Truly in the midst of life we are in death.

On July 2d, we moved from our position at Malvern Hill to Harrison's Landing, to which point the Federals had retreated to the shelter of their gun boats; on the 3d some skirmishing occurred, as also on the following days. We remained in his front for four or five days. The storm and downpour of rain the day after Malvern Hill in its discomforts and injury to the army, ammunition and stores was distressing. Preceding and following this storm the beaming sun heated the humid atmosphere and made the army as miserable as well could be, but relief soon came in our removal to the Mechanicsville road near Richmond. Here we were free from mosquito ridden marshes and poison laden atmosphere, endured for half a month, in daily battle, the march and duties of soldiers in active war.

The seven days' battles were ended and had resulted in freeing the Capital City of immediate menace. McClellan at the head of his splendid army of over 110,000 well-equipped soldiers at its gates for many months perfecting plans for entrance over the opposition of 63,000 Confederates under Johnston, had been beaten, swept back and left in no condition to renew the effort. This relief of Richmond was contributed to by the battle of Seven Pines of May 23. Before that time – as stated in accounts and reports – "McClellan had advanced his left wing consisting of two of his five corps from his position on the north of the Chickahominy to the south of that stream, heavy spring rains had converted the streams into torrents, his military bridges across the Chickahominy into trembling and swaying structures, and the mud and mire made the movement and use of his heavy artillery practically impossible. The astute Johnston saw McClellan's faulty position, and availed himself of the opportunity to attack his left wing on May 23d. He drove it from the field and back more than a mile, capturing many prisoners, a number of pieces of artillery, small arms and a number of tents."

Unfortunately Johnston was struck by a fragment of shell late in the afternoon of the first day, knocked from his horse, and carried from the field in an insensible condition. Major-General G.W. Smith succeeded to command. McClellan had gotten Sumner's Corps to his left wing, and thus reinforced the Federals entrenched their position, and the battles of the succeeding days amounted to

little more than skirmishes and were without material results. The treacherous Chickahominy now intervened between McClellan's two corps on the
north and his three corps on the south of that stream.
This position was so held June 26, at the time of the
advance of Lee, who had been assigned to the command of the army on the first day of that month.

There can be no question but that Johnston's
attack was wise and successful, not only because he
won the day, but because he drew a large part of
McClellan's right wing from the north to the south
of the Chickahominy, thus leaving much less than
half of the Federal army on the north of the river,
and contributing to Lee's success against this iso-
lated right wing. At this time McClellan's entire
army must have aggregated 110,000 to 115,000. In
the early part of May his force was placed at
110,000. Lee's entire army, including Jackson, was
80,000 to 85,000. With this inferior force in numbers much was accomplished, yet with the attending
advantages greater results might have been attained.
There does not seem to have been any fault in Lee's
plans or leadership; but fault, if such existed, must
have been lack of cooperation by the separate commands.

Yet unforeseen conditions may have prevented this. Lee risked much when he withdrew his
main army from Richmond to the north of the
Chickahominy, leaving but 25,000 men under Magruder to defend the city against more than twice to
three times their number of the best of McClellan's

army; but this, of course, was considered by Lee, and results justified his course. The victories of the seven days were substantial, except Malvern Hill, which, except for the freeing of Richmond, nearly offset the previous six days. The attack on such a position so manned and garrisoned was a mistake.

CHAPTER EIGHT

Advance Against Pope. Battle at Cedar Run.
Battle at Bristoe Station. Battle at Manassas.
Battles Near Groveton on 28-29th.
Battle Renewed on 30th.

About the 1st of August, Jackson's corps moved toward Gordonsville. When the troops got under way and the head of the column had been turned sharply to the left, indicating the direction of our march toward the mountains and the valley, where pure air and good water could be had, a shout arose that was deafening in its volume; and it was taken up by the column as it reached the turn, and was so continued until the corps had passed.

The same occurred, except possibly in greater volume, on the following day when the Blue Ridge was first brought into view. This elevation of spirits, pure air, and drinkable water soon made the army itself again.

The head of the column, however, soon

turned toward Culpeper Court House; and, on the 9th, Pope's advance was found in position on Cedar Run, at the northwest base of Slaughter Mountain, about eight miles from Culpeper Court House. Our guns were soon placed and about 2 p.m. a heavy artillery duel opened and continued for about two hours. The batteries of Poag, of Carpenter and of Caskie were well placed and appeared to do fine execution. Our brigade supported these batteries, which, of course, were targets for the enemy's guns, as was the brigade. In the meantime, the infantry was being brought into position near the brow of a low ridge. Our brigade occupied the line to the left of Early's, and to the right of the second brigade of Jackson's division About 4 p.m., the line advanced over the ridge into an open wheat field. Two hundred yards to our front was thick timber and undergrowth. From the timber the enemy advanced in great numbers, forcing back the brigade to our left. This compelled the "3rd Brigade" also to fall back to meet this flank and rear attack, but again as soon as our left was sufficiently protected by A.P. Hill the whole line moved forward and turned the Federal right and the day was practically won. Federal cavalry in great force charged on our brigade, but was repulsed with heavy loss.

A brilliant dash on our right of our flying artillery was beautifully executed in view of both armies and did splendid work. Our whole line now pushed forward, and the Federals gave way at every point in confusion and disorder, leaving their dead

and wounded on the field. General Winder, commanding our division, was struck by a piece of shell
during the artillery duel and died in a few minutes.
He occupied a high place in the esteem of the army
and the loss was deeply felt.

Other incidents occurred during this artillery
duel. A shell exploded in the ranks of a regiment and
five men fell to death together and upon each other.
Our losses in this battle, as shown by statistics, were
19 officers killed and 114 wounded, of non-commis-
sioned officers and privates 204 killed and 946
wounded and 31 missing, aggregating a loss of 1,314.
The Federal loss was greater. "The regiment" had its
due share of casualties, owing to its prominent share
in the engagement. After more than forty-five years
it is impossible to recall the names of the unfortunates,
but I do recall that Capt. John Duff of Company "C"
and I were in conversation just as we reached the
border of the wheat field from the skirt of the woods.
He was in a most cheerful mood as we entered this
rapid and fierce battle. He fell in death a few minutes
after he entered. Capt. Felix Duff of Company "H,"
another brave and efficient officer, fell mortally
wounded and died in a few hours. I was of the number
of the wounded. Of the killed and wounded of the
regiment I am unable to recall the number, names or
companies, except in one instance, and that was impressed upon my mind because of the nature of the
wound and of the unlooked for result, viz: Young
Combs of Company "C" was to appearances vigorous
and strong, of fine physical appearance. It was his first

first battle. A minnie ball passed just under the skin in the calf of the leg for the space of one or two inches and out. There was but little blood, no artery had been touched and no reason could be assigned for serious results; nevertheless, he was greatly excited and died in a few minutes.

The victory over superior numbers by Jackson's army, composed of the divisions of Jackson, Early and A.P. Hill, had a telling effect; but now the Federal Commander, Pope, who had so valiantly proclaimed headquarters in the saddle, began to concentrate his army on a strong position near Culpeper Court House to resist Jackson's further advance. But Jackson chose to await the coming of the main army under Lee which was still in the vicinity of Richmond, hence retired to Gordonsville.

The rest and recuperation so much needed was now enjoyed until the middle of August, thus putting the army in fine condition for the campaign then entered upon. The route of which was by way of Orange Court House, thence up the right bank of Rapidan River. The divisions of Ewell, Hill and Jackson composed Jackson's corps, and on the 12th moved in the direction of Beverly Ford on the Rappahannock. Jackson's division, now commanded by Talliaferro, was at the head of the column. In the afternoon a spirited artillery duel across the river was fought, resulting in the silencing of the Federals, who, however, brought forward and began to concentrate a strong force. The river still separating these armies, the Confederates continued the march up the right bank, the head of the column crossing on the 24th to the left bank. The balance of the corps, strung out for many miles, followed in the wake of the advance, encountering on the way like artillery duels across the river, but not swerved from the end sought, pushed forward for a week with but little sleep or rest toward the rear of Pope's army, and at Salem Church went into bivouac for the night. On the following day, the march being continued across Bull Run Mountain through Thoroughfare Gap and Gainesville to Bristoe Station on the railroad, we were now in the rear of Pope and between his army and Washington. Here some prisoners and loaded cars were captured, and the same night at Manassas, seven miles distant, a number of prisoners, cannon, small arms, ammunition, immense and valuable commissary and quartermaster stores were captured.

On the 27th, a force came from the direction of Washington, hoping to regain the captured stores and prisoners, made a vigorous attack and contested the field with much vigor for some hours, but were in the end defeated, routed, and disappeared, leaving their dead and wounded on the field. In the afternoon of the same day, the Federals in full force attacked the Confederates at Bristoe Station from the direction of Warrenton. The battle raged fierce and furious. The Federals were repulsed. The Confederates were now withdrawn to the army at Manassas.

The following day, the 28th, the Confederates took position toward Groveton on the Warrenton and Alexandria Turnpike. The Federals in full force were now moving on the Confederates from the direction of Warrenton, hoping to crush them before Lee, with the main army, could reach the field. An effort to move a large part of this force to the east of the Confederates, and thus intervene between them and Washington, exposed his left flank, upon which Jackson with his comparatively small army, without the slightest hesitation, made a vigorous assault, which continued with great spirit until about nine o'clock at night, the Federals being pushed back from the field. By the following morning, the 29th, it was found that the enemy had moved his position further to our left with the evident purpose of covering the way to the Federal Capital, and about ten a.m. opened with artillery a vigorous attack upon our right, which was repulsed by the Confederate batteries at the end of about two hours. A lull now followed, interrupted only by an occasional artillery shot, until about 2 p.m. The Federal infantry in heavy force now made a vigorous attack on the Confederate left. This was beaten back, as were successive attacks by fresh relays of troops, until the Confederates, exhausted and out of ammunition, were forced back three or four hundred yards, their line broken and a part of the force cut off. At this supreme moment reinforcements from the right arrived and engaged the victorious enemy with grim determination. The battle, now more furious than before, swayed to and fro; and for sometime doubtful conclusions hung in the balance. The enemy continued to pour in his fresh relays, which were met by the same grim veterans of many battles. The contest constantly grew fiercer and more bloody. Often the combatants delivered their fire against each other within ten or a dozen paces.

This awful carnage could not continue long. The slaughter was too horrible and sickening. The tide must turn, and it did. At the supreme moment in battle a word, a slight act, may, and often does, decide the fate of the day. At this supreme moment an officer, or private, as has been claimed, in the very forefront of the closest quarters, called out in a lusty voice, "Charge 'em, boys, charge 'em." This was the needed stimulant. It nerved the heart and hand of the weary Confederates and was responded to by the whole line with such unanimous vigor and force that the enemy was swept from the field with great loss. The Confederate loss was also heavy. "The Regiment" and the Confederates reoccupied the stronger line held by them at the beginning.

On the following day, the 30th, cannonading and some skirmishing occurred until about 4 o'clock. The enemy began to advance in a number of successive lines. Soon the battle became sanguinary and determined and extended along the entire front. The Confederates on the left occupied a favorable position and repulsed the onslaught made upon them. As one line was repulsed a fresh one took its place, and thus the battle raged over the dead and wounded Federals who fell on this oft' traversed field. The main Confederate army, which had now reached the field, and Jackson's worn and decimated corps were now contesting the field with a brave army of superior numbers; but a change of conditions must come, and again the psychological moment arrived and was availed of by the Confederates, pressed to the last inch of endurance. Our right now held by Longstreet pressed the enemy back. This invigorated the whole Confederate line, which now with eager and invincible will simultaneously joined in the forward movement and pressed upon the still stubborn and equally determined foe, resisting with bayonet the onward rush; but the tide turned against the Federals and they fled precipitately, leaving their dead and wounded on the field. The Confederates now opened upon the fleeing Federals and their loss at this time, as during the day, was very heavy. The Confederate loss was also heavy. A number of pieces of artillery and many stands of small arms fell into the hands of the Confederates. The enemy continued his retreat.

Pursuit was taken up by Jackson's corps in the lead and, on the 1st of September, the enemy in force was again encountered at Ox Hill. Here a sanguinary battle of much fury occurred, lasting for some time, when a heavy storm brought a cessation of the contest for a time, during which the enemy retired about night and by the next morning had disappeared. On the following day, the 3d, Jackson's corps moved toward Loudoun county and on the 4th went into bivouac near Leesburg.

CHAPTER NINE

☆ ☆ ☆ ☆

Capture of Harper's Ferry. Battle of Sharpsburg.
Return to Virginia. Battle of Fredericksburg.

About the 5th of September, Jackson's corps
crossed the Potomac into Maryland near Leesburg,
moving toward Frederick, Md.; and on or about the
10th moved toward Martinsburg, recrossing the Potomac near Williamsport. On the following day, the
course was down the right bank of the Potomac toward Harpers Ferry, near which on Bolivar Heights
a Federal force under General Miles was hemmed in
by the Confederates who occupied Maryland and
Loudoun heights and all the passes leading out from
the Federal position. In the contest little else occurred than artillery firing, which continued for
about two hours, resulting in but few casualties on
either side. Realizing their inextricable position, the
Federals "on the morning of the 15th surrendered
unconditionally all the force, consisting of approximately 12,000 men, 74 pieces of artillery, many thou-

sands of small arms and large military stores." The details of the surrender were left with A. P. Hill's division to adjust while the balance of Jackson's corps left in haste for Sharpsburg, where Longstreet and D. H. Hill were already engaged with the enemy, who by greatly superior numbers had forced the passes of South Mountain, causing the Confederates to take position near Sharpsburg behind Antietam Creek on the morning of the 15th. Early on the morning of the 16th, Jackson's corps, except Hill's division, arrived.

On the afternoon of the 15th, the enemy had advanced and the batteries on both sides were immediately engaged. On the 16th, artillery firing continued during the entire day. Jackson's old division occupied the left from Hagerstown road to the Potomac. At dawn on the 17th, the enemy's artillery opened with great vigor on Jackson's line. The battle was hot and furious from the start and continued for many hours with alternate success. The Federal lines were forced back several times, but new lines of fresh troops were met, and in turn the Confederates were forced to retire before them, but would again return to the contest and again clear their front, only to be again pushed back as before. This was the part of the Confederate line against which the enemy had concentrated and was now hurling the strength of his army, and by overwhelming numbers turning the Confederates left; but reinforcements from our right arrived in time, and now the battle raged with still greater fury and determination. But the onslaught of the Confederates was not to be successfully resisted, hence they swept the Federals back and reestablished their lines, which were held against further attacks of the day. Between these hostile lines lay hundreds of dead and dying of both sides, fighting being so continuous as to prevent proper attention to them. I do not now recall the names of any of these, except that of a younger brother, the late Judge M. B. Wood, whose wound was severe, and naturally I was impressed. The main attack was now shifted from our left to the center. This was finally repulsed and the battle along the line was now reduced to a more moderate degree; heavy attacks, however, were made occasionally on different parts of the Confederate lines. Hill arrived from Harpers Ferry late in the afternoon and attacked the enemy on our right, and drove him from his position back across Antietam, inflicting much loss.

On the morning of the 18th, the Confederates held their entire lines and awaited an advance by the enemy, he having superior numbers and equipment; but he did not advance. That night, owing to the enemy being about to receive large reinforcements as was then understood, and the rains which had fallen causing a rise in the Potomac which would thus cut off the Confederates from their base of supplies, Lee withdrew his army to the Virginia side, crossing at Shepardstown without loss. The best that could be claimed by either side was that the battle was a draw; neither side won.

Jackson's division went into camp at Bunker's Hill, twelve miles below Winchester, and here received much needed rest, food, clothing and shoes. After a short time of drill, picket, guard and camp duty, recuperation ensued; the arduous and perilous duties of the Maryland campaign were forgotten and the army was itself again. Here our division remained until October, then moved to the vicinity of Berryville, thence across the Blue Ridge to camp near Guiny's Station.

On the morning of December 12th, the division moved in much haste to Hamilton's Crossing, four miles below Fredericksburg. It was then known that the Federal army under command of General Burnside was crossing the Rappahannock at and below that city. Many advantages seemed to favor the enterprise. Of these were his many well placed long range guns on Stafford Heights from opposite the city to Hamilton's Crossing, a distance of four miles, completely dominating and commanding the lower range of hills on the Confederate side far back from the river. His greatly superior numbers and equipment gave promise of success to his advance. Pontoon bridges at Fredericksburg, at Hamilton's Crossing and points between, completely protected by the high river banks from shot and shell, enabled him to transfer his army expeditiously to the west side, between which and the ridge – occupied by the Confederates – is a smooth open plain, varying in width from one to one and a half miles and extending in length from the city to below Hamilton's Crossing, a distance of more than four miles. This topography rendered it impracticable for the Confederates to maintain a force at or near the river or on this open plain to dispute the crossing by the enemy.

On the morning of the 11th, Burnside opened on the Confederates with about one hundred and fifty guns from Stafford Heights, and advanced to the river a large infantry force, thus compelling the Confederate pickets to retire. The enemy then proceeded to construct his pontoon crossings, and during the night and following day, being protected by a dense fog as well as high river banks, crossed his army. Little occurred on the following day, except occasional artillery firing at the Confederate position from Stafford Heights, as rifts would occur in the dense fog which still hung over the field. This firing was not returned by the Confederates, but as occasional clearings of the fog would reveal the enemy's columns on the plain a vigorous and apparently effective fire was opened upon them. Of the Confederates, Longstreet occupied the left, including Mary's and Willis' Hills, and Jackson the right, extending to Hamilton's Crossing; the extreme right being protected by Stuart's cavalry. The first and second lines of battle, the reserves and the artillery now in position, awaited the advance of the enemy which did not occur that day. On the morning of the 13th, the plain now occupied by the Federals was still enveloped in dense fog. About 10 o'clock, the fog cleared and the lines of the enemy in order of battle could be seen upon the plain between the Confederate position and the river, in front of our position at Hamilton's Crossing and extending miles to our left toward Fredericksburg. The force in front of Jackson's corps alone was estimated at not less than 50,000.

Federal batteries from Stafford Heights opened fire upon the Confederate lines, the heaviest of which was directed against the line far to our left, toward the city, to which the Confederates did not reply, but held their fire for the infantry, now advancing in numerous lines of battle against our front. At our position A. P. Hill's division was in front, and Jackson's division in the second or supporting line, and our artillery was well placed. In addition to the batteries of the enemy on Stafford Heights, some of his field batteries on the plain and a battery of the Confederates on our right engaged in a duel which continued with great spirit for more than an hour, when the Confederates withdrew and the enemy now advanced unmolested, turning his batteries on our position. The Confederates reserved their fire until the Federal lines came within easy range before they opened, pouring such a storm of shot and shell into his ranks as to cause him to waver and then to retreat in confusion and disorder.

A comparative lull now ensued until about 2 o'clock, when the Federals made a furious artillery attack, inflicting great damage on our lines. Under the protection of this fire, his infantry in heavy force again advanced. When, as before, they had gotten within easy range, our batteries opened fire on him with destructive effect. Though staggered and shocked by this rapid and well directed fire, their lines regained composure, continued to press forward and soon came within easy range of our infantry lines. Then the conflict at once began with great fury. Musketry and artillery continued to play upon his ranks with withering effect, but still he pressed forward; and, finding a gap in our line some distance to our left, – open by accident, – he pressed through in great numbers, and now pressing in front, as well as the flanks, the advantage was with the Federals. But the Confederates with heroic desperation continued the contest, but were forced to yield ground. Thus the breach widened and the enemy in still greater numbers pressed on, still the battle raged. The dead and dying on both sides lay intermingled on the field with no hope of assistance to the wounded, until the battle should end. Yet dead and dying continued to fall thick and fast. The day now seemed almost lost to the Confederates. Decimated, worn and almost without ammunition, they still bitterly contested the advance of the Federals. At this time the Confederate reserves reached the field and at once made descent on this victorious force with such impetuosity that it was swept back and our lines advanced farther than before, going to the edge of the plain along the railroad. The enemy did not advance again during the day, but kept up at intervals his artillery fire. The simultaneous attack on the Confederate lines to the left of Jackson's corps was equally fierce and determined, and quite as sanguinary, and perhaps more so at Mary's and Willis' Hills. Six times did the enemy attack these positions, and each of these attacks was repulsed with great loss. The Confederates also lost heavily here, as well as at other parts of the line. The work of the day was now over. Our division now occupied the railroad, this being the front line.

During the day incidents too numerous to mention occurred, one or two of which impressed me. While moving to position under heavy shelling, a soldier from the line in front came obliquely toward the left and rear. He wore a very long sandy beard and carried his gun in his left hand at his side. The boys began to guy him for getting to the rear. "You are safer in ranks," "Fortune favors the brave," "You are skulking," and so on went this fusillade against this poor, downcast looking man, during which an exploding shell struck him and he was literally no more. A little farther on we discovered a soldier who had taken refuge behind a large oak tree, lying in apparent security, but a shell had struck the ground in front of the tree, passed under it, came out and exploded, tearing him into bits. Thus Fate seemed to have attended them. Another, but more pleasing scene, occurred soon after nightfall. The survivors of that field of both armies will remember, if for no other reason than the relief it gave by transference of thought and attention from the carnage of the day, and now irresistibly fixed them on an aurora borealis, or northern light. This at first appeared as a dimly reflected light from below the horizon, but it continued to grow in brightness and volume until it covered a wide space against the sky, and then shooting up its steady and well defined columns, each tinted in separate and distinct hues, ascended to a great height, and thus continued for many minutes, then all gradually faded away, never to be pictured to others by brush or pen. The awe and beauty of this natural apparition as it appeared on that night of December 13th, 1862, will ever hold a place in memory.

Jackson's and Early's divisions remained on the front line at the railroad during that night and the following day. The Federals also remained in line of battle all day as if expecting attack, but an attack by the Confederates was impossible, because the well-placed guns on Stafford Heights could and would have swept from the broad open plain any force that might have attempted to cross it. This could have been done by the Federals more effectually by reason of his superior position and number of guns than our own artillery had done on his advancing columns, on the day before. Neither side advanced during the day, and nothing save some desultory artillery firing occurred. During the night our division was relieved by D.H. Hill and we were moved back to a position in the line of reserves. During the 15th the enemy remained in battle array, as if still looking for attack; but in the afternoon sent in a flag of truce and a request for permission to take his wounded from the field. This was granted, after which not even an artillery shot – so frequent before – was heard; deathlike stillness prevailed. Our troops were in fine spirits and only hoped the enemy would come out of his stronghold on the following day and again attack. This he did not do, but on the night of the 15th, re-crossed the river and thus ended the prospect of further contest.

We now returned to camp and established winter quarters on the Rappahannock at Buckner's Neck. The routine of camp life was entered upon and the exercising from daily drill and other duties, better food, shoes and clothing, gave contentment, and the army was soon restored to fine condition. Picket duty on the river during the winter brought the troops of the opposing armies into such close proximity that a continual battle across the river could have been kept up, but instead a tacit armistice was maintained between the soldiers themselves. This was done by neither pen or tongue, but simply by acts, developing into such a kindly feeling that frequently in the absence of officers interchange of visits were made by crossing the river on improvised rafts for the exchange of tobacco from the Confederates for coffee from the Federals. This occurred daily. An incident of the kind came under my own observation while in command of the picket force, the reserve post of which was stationed back, and smaller posts stationed nearer to different eligible crossings, along and near the river bank. The same arrangement seemed to be true of the Federal pickets, and it was between these lines that intercourse orally and commercially existed. In passing down the river along this line I discovered a small improvised craft of bark provided with newspaper sails gliding to the Federal side with its plainly seen lading. My duty was to investigate and have arrested the violators of this plain breach of discipline. Although regarded as a disciplinarian, I could not find it in my heart to do this, accord and harmony being too inviolable to be disturbed when material damage therefrom did not portend; and as nothing of the kind threatened here I simply failed to see or know of the little craft.

On a recent call at my home of an ex-Federal captain, Charles P. Tanner, and his estimable wife, I related the above to him and he in turn related a kindred experience of this period. He was then in the ranks and was possessed of this fellow-feeling as were his comrades. He said that by means of improvised rafts the Federals and Confederates would exchange visits in the absence of the officers in charge. On one of these visits to the Confederates a comrade and himself, being of sporting proclivities, engaged in a game of cards with the Confederates which soon became interesting and absorbing to those engaged and the others standing by as well. At this time the Confederate officer in charge had approached unobserved until he made demand of the Federals to know what they were doing there and did they not know that this intercourse was against the orders of the commanders of both armies? Well knowing such orders, but not admitting the same, the Federals adroitly inquired, "What orders?" An explanation followed with an admonition to the Federals to get to their own side of the river. It is needless to say that the admonition was heeded. The evening thus spent with this liberal minded and estimable gentleman, in which many other reminiscences so common to both were gone over, was quite enjoyable.

About the middle of April, 1863, the Federals made a demonstration at Port Royal, twelve miles below our camp, by crossing the Rappahannock at that place with a small part of his army. The "3rd Brigade" was hurried there, but the Federals returned to the east side before our arrival. No further demonstration at this point was made, but we remained there for some days, enjoying the fine shad, so abundant in the Rappahannock in the then shad season.

CHAPTER TEN

Federal Advance. Flank Movement of
Confederates. Attack on Federal Right Rear.
Jackson Wounded. Battle of Chancellorsville.
Jackson's Death.

About this time the Federals made demonstration at Kelley's Ford, some miles above Fredericksburg. The two armies had been lying on opposite sides of this river, since the battle of Fredericksburg in December. Gen. Joe Hooker was now in command of the Federal army, and on the 28th of April a small part of his army crossed the river a little below Fredericksburg, thus indicating an intended advance from that direction.

This, however, as were other demonstrations, was for the purpose of drawing attention from his real course of approach, which soon developed to be by way of the United States and other fords of the Rappahannock, fifteen and twenty miles above Fredericksburg, where he crossed his army and was bearing down by way of Chancellorsville upon Lee's left and rear. Here the Federals encountered Anderson's and McLaw's divisions, and thinking it an advance by Lee took a formidable defensive position, extending his lines from the Furnace and Tabernacle Church to Chancellorsville, thence behind Mineral Spring Run to and beyond the old Mine Road.

This strong position and the superior numbers of the Federals put the consideration of a front attack out of the question, but the emergency was great and had to be met; but how? Longstreet's corps was away and the inadequacy of numbers was great and conditions serious. But Jackson, as usual, cut the gordian knot. In answer to the query of Lee, as to what should be done, he replied, "Outflank them." This was accepted as the best solution, and Jackson was entrusted with this important task. On the morning of May 1st, he set out with his old division commanded by General Colston, A.P. Hill's and Rodes' divisions. This was a great risk for Lee to divide his army in the front of his advancing antagonist for this great flank movement. It was contrary to the principles of strategy for Jackson to take his corps of 26,000 men, leaving Lee with about 18,000 men an easy prey, to be crushed by Hooker, who could then turn upon Jackson with his entire army; but Hooker did not know conditions or did not avail of the opportunity thus presented. He also certainly blundered in failing to properly protect his right wing, but for this failure of Hooker success would hardly have attended Jackson's move. The disparity in numbers and position in favor of the Federals was too great.

Our course was up the old turnpike to within a mile or two of Chancellorsville, thence directly to the left over a country road, passing along the immediate rear of Anderson's division, then in line of battle and now receiving shots from the advancing Federals, thence to the left by the old Furnace, moving in great haste. We thus made the impression on the Federals that it was the beginning of a precipitate retreat. Thus encouraged, the enemy made an overwhelming assault upon Anderson, pressed him back and captured some of Jackson's ammunition train; but on we sped, soon turning to the right, making our course due north. The day was excessively hot and many fell by the way from heat and exhaustion. We reached and crossed the Orange Plank Road leading to Chancellorsville, then the Culpeper Plank Road; next we reached a county road and formed line of battle across this road about 5 o'clock in the afternoon, facing Chancellorsville to the southeast. We were now in the rear of the enemy's right. Our advance began between five and six o'clock. We soon struck Howard's corps, which gave way in precipitous rout. Fresh troops and impediments were utterly unable to stop or seriously impede our onward sweep. We captured prisoners, artillery and small arms on the way, but steadily continued the pursuit until darkness and the deep tangled undergrowth put an end to further advance.

We were now within a mile of Chancellorsville. A skirmish line was thrown out and moved forward to within less than half a mile of the enemy's position. Our brigade and others followed in formation of two columns occupying the respective sides of the Plank Road, and a column of artillery occupied the middle, with the third brigade at the head of one of the columns. Our skirmish line extended across our front a hundred yards ahead. The enemy was in his strong position awaiting attack. Like the calm before the storm, quiet and stillness now reigned, except with the ever vigilant Jackson. Intent on investigating conditions in his front he passed through our skirmish line accompanied by his staff, and after making reconnoissance returned to another point toward the Confederate skirmish line. This surprise brought a fire from the skirmish line and then from the enemy, who thought it an attack. Hence he opened fire upon us with a fury that was hardly surpassed, if equalled, during the war. Shot, shell, grape and cannister tore through the ranks of men and artillery horses. Minnie balls came like hail in a spring storm. Exploding shells would kill some and wound many. Solid shot would plough through the ranks, leaving a line of dead and dying. Grape and cannister would slay and wound groups and squads, while minnie did an effective but indiscriminate work of destruction. Caissons of ammunition were blown up by exploding shells, adding to the work of destruction. Added to this was the plunging and leaping of wounded artillery horses, thus increasing the peril to life. The horribleness of that dark night is indescribable. It was not a battle, but a firing by the Federals. The Confederates could do nothing but protect themselves as best they could by lying upon the ground. They were not in formation to engage in battle, nor could they withdraw; because to arise was to be cut down like grass before the mower's scythe. This may be figurative, but there is no question but many lives were saved by lying upon the ground until the end.

Jackson had been wounded and in the midst of this fusillade litter bearers had placed him upon a litter and one at each of the four corners raised him to their shoulders and started from the field. Soon one of the bearers was stricken down, causing Jackson to fall heavily to the ground. His wounds were not thought to be serious, the bone of the left arm a few inches below the shoulder and the cutting of the artery in the arm being the principal injury. This occurred on Saturday night, May 1. Before dawn of the following day, amputation of the arm was performed and the patient revived and gave every evidence of recovery, but finally pneumonia supervened, and on the following Sunday the great Chieftain, at the age of thirty-seven, triumphantly passed into the Great Beyond. Great gloom was cast over the whole army and the people of the South. When he was wounded all watched with deep anxiety and prayerful hearts for his restoration the sick bed of this illustrious patient, and when the end came grief was sincere and profound. He left as a heritage to his country an unblemished life of Christian devotion, pure patriotism and great deeds. Jackson will ever live in the hearts of his people.

After the fusillade of that night – May the 1st – the troops were removed a little farther to the rear and formed into line of battle, and thus went into bivouac for the balance of the night. By 10 o'clock on the following morning the advance on the enemy's strong position began. Jackson's old division constituted a part of the front line. We passed through thick undergrowth until we reached the crest of a low ridge. At this point and in our front the undergrowth had been cut away and the enemy was posted behind well-constructed breast works of logs, stone and earth on the face of a corresponding but higher ridge. Between these positions a sluggish streamlet formed a bog about fifty or more yards wide, and extending a long distance across our front to the right and to the left. This bog had been well studded with tough white oak saplings which had been felled, leaving them uncut from the stump, and so crossed and piled as to make, when added to the bog itself, the mud and slush of which was one or more feet deep, an almost impenetrable obstruction. From higher grounds, back of his lines, the enemy threw shell, solid shot, grape and cannister into our position with great fury, but being fairly well protected by the crest of the ridge our casualties were not very great.

Before our advance Lieut. Walter S. Preston was sitting near me, leaning against a small sapling. We saw a solid six-pound shot rolling slowly down the hill toward us and before Preston could get entirely out of its way, it brushed by his shoulder. It did not strike him, but the concussion and force was so much greater than thought and the effect so much more serious that he was disabled for a long time. Here, too, Major Walker of the 10th Virginia Regiment, my personal friend and with whom I was conversing at the time, while sitting on a stump, was struck by a shell and instantly killed. Many other casualties at this point occurred in my company and regiment, but I do not recall the names. The advance was now ordered, and inasmuch as no troops could have stood and exchanged shots with the Federals, his artillery and infantry being so well protected by breastworks, there was nothing that promised success but to charge down the decline and across this formidable bog and onto the enemy in his stronghold.

This was done with great gallantry by the entire Confederate lines, led by Gen. J. E. B. Stuart in person, he now being in immediate command of Jackson's corps, the latter and A. P. Hill, next in rank, both having been wounded and disabled. We received the fusillade of infantry and artillery fire, so furious that it seemed that but few would be left to tell the tale. But little firing was done by the Confederates, as rapid movement so necessary prevented.

Our progress across the bog was unavoidably slower, but we soon emerged therefrom and ascended the slope in fine mood for effective work, drove the enemy from his line of works and in turn as he retreated in great haste across the plateau inflicted heavy damage upon him, strewing the field with his dead and dying. He, however, returned with fresh lines to retake the works, but was repulsed with loss. By this time, however, the Confederate line some distance to our left gave way, and the enemy in strong force penetrated through the gap to the left rear of our position and opened a vigorous fire upon us. Being thus assailed in front and rear, we were ordered to relinquish the costly position we had gained and again recross the bog and ascend the incline under a galling fire from two directions. Our damage, of course, was heavy, but the spirit of our army was undaunted.

The broken part of our lines were soon restored with fresh troops and we again returned to the charge. This time we knew it could be done and with swiftness and determination swept down to and across the bog and on the works, and again returned kind for kind with good interest on our retreating foe, who soon again with fresh lines made a beautiful and gallant effort to retake the works, advancing his rapidly melting lines to within a short distance. But the fire upon him was so destructive that he was compelled to retire. Our part of the Confederate line prematurely advanced in pursuit, but when we reached the highest part of the plateau, we met such a storm of shot, shell, grape, cannister and minnies from different directions – we being the only part of the lines exposed, – that we were compelled to return to the works.

Our whole lines were now lined up and again advanced. Our part of the line again met the enemy's fire on the plateau and here, as before, we met a brave and stubborn resistance which continued for some time. Our own, as well as many of the enemy's ranks, melted away rapidly, but in the grim determination of the contending armies the battle raged. On this disputed ground the undergrowth had been cleared away, but the trees and saplings had been left standing. Many of the latter, including in one instance a tree of considerable size, were cut down by minnie balls. McLaw's division now came into position on the right and a general charge along the line was made. The enemy gave way and the battle of Sunday, the 2nd of May, was ended.

The losses of both sides were heavy over the whole field. On this disputed plateau the dead of the two armies must have lain within an average of five or six feet, or even less, all over that broad space, as my memory now serves me. The enemy now pursued by the Confederates retired to his last line of fortifications, about three miles back toward the United States Ford. In the meantime the enemy, under Sedgwick with superior numbers, had pressed back the Confederates at Fredericksburg about five miles toward our position at Chancellorsville, thus seriously threatening our rear. This forced Lee to withdraw several divisions of his army, confronting Hooker at Chancellorsville, and to meet and drive across the river this triumphant advance of Sedgwick; which was done.

This left but the three divisions of Jackson's corps to hold our front at Chancellorsville. The writer was placed in charge of the picket line in our front on the night of the 3rd, and there remained until the morning of the 6th. In the meantime firing by the opposing picket lines was frequent, resulting in many casualties. About midnight of the 5th, I thought movements of the enemy indicated the beginning of his withdrawal, and at once so reported. I was directed to watch further developments and report; and soon being satisfied the enemy was rapidly withdrawing, I so reported and was directed to advance on his works at daylight. This I did and found the works vacated, on the report of which I was directed to assemble my battalion and pursue. I threw out a skirmish line covering our front for some distance on each side of the road, and moved on the road toward the United States Ford, followed by Jackson's old division and other troops. Here the enemy had crossed the river on his pontoon bridges, well guarded by his numerous artillery. Under flag of truce he was permitted to send a detail to bury his dead. Both armies were now quiet for some days.

The preceding strenuous days were full of interesting events. On the morning of the 1st, after we had gotten under way on the march to the rear of the enemy, a soldier of the writer's company told some of his comrades that he was to be killed that day. They tried to laugh him out of the premonition, but he said it had come to him too plainly and forcibly, and further that no power could save him from the pending fate that he would encounter in the battle which would occur that day. His comrades thought lightly of it, but

the battle began about 5 p.m. We advanced very rapidly. James P. Walling, who still lives, was at my left
and James Warf, the subject of this event, at my
right. We were a little to the front of the line. A dis-
charge of grape from one of the enemy's guns to our
left sent a grape through the right arm of Walling
and another into the left side of Warf. He fell lifeless
to the ground; and thus his premonition was ful-
filled, of which premonition I was not apprised until
after the battle, or he would have been excused from
the fight. These shots must have passed within an
inch or less of my body, one in front, the other at the
back. Such occurrences, however, were frequent. On
the second day of the battle (Sunday morning) I received a slight wound in the left side, but did not
leave the field nor quit duty. If my memory is not at
fault, my company numbered forty-two men when
we entered the battle on Sunday morning, and at the
end of the conflict it numbered sixteen. Nearly two-
thirds had been killed or disabled, not including
some who had received slight wounds but did not
quit the field, and were hence not counted among
the wounded. In looking back on this battle I can but
consider it one of the most remarkable victories
gained by the Confederates during the war.

Gen. Joe Hooker, a brave and skillful general,
had been placed in command of the Federal army.
During the winter preceding his advance he had
perfected its organization, equipment and discipline
to a very high degree. Nothing was lacking. His plan
of advance and attack, considering his superiority of

numbers and equipment, promised success. He selected crossings of the river where the banks on the Confederate side were low and well dominated by the higher grounds on the other side, and where there was no force to dispute his crossing. On the way to Chancellorsville and beyond there were no strong positions to be occupied by the Confederates. His army led by able lieutenants seemed to offer every prospect of turning the Confederate left and driving him back on Richmond. It was a gigantic flank movement in which his entire army, except Sedgwick's corps which was left opposite Fred-ericksburg, was employed. His entire force numbered 95,000 men, while Lee's army numbered 46,000 including Stuart's cavalry of 3,000. Nearly one-fourth of his army was not available for this emergency, Longstreet's corps being on duty below Richmond. It was the beginning of the spring campaign and the troops on both sides were fresh and in fine trim. All went well with Hooker until he reached Chancellorsville and encountered Anderson's and a part of McLaw's divisions. Thinking this to be Lee's advance, he took a strong defensive position, but when he saw Jackson's forces early in the day and before the engagement marching along at the back of Anderson's and McLaw's men, he evidently mistook it for the beginning of a retreat and made a vigorous attack on McLaw's and Anderson, forcing them back some distance. But Jackson kept on until he passed around Hooker's exposed right, and what followed has already been related. After the battle, Lee's army went into camp within striking distance of Fredericksburg, opposite to which the Federals again took position.

Maj. Henry Clinton Wood
photograph taken 1896

CHAPTER ELEVEN

☆ ☆ ☆ ☆

Return to the Valley. Battle at Winchester.
Crossed the Potomac. Battle at Gettysburg.
Charge of Hays and Hoke.
Charge of 3rd Brigade.

Early in June, Jackson's, now Ewell's corps, took up the march to the valley, passing through the Blue Ridge, crossing the Shenandoah River at Front Royal. From here Johnston's division, to which my brigade and regiment belonged, moved over the Front Royal road, while Early's division moved over the valley pike, on Winchester, now occupied by a Federal force under General Milroy. Johnston's division took position on the south and engaged the attention of the enemy, while Early moved to the north and by rapid and skilful movement captured the heights that dominated the fort and works of the enemy and made them untenable, but too late to complete the work of reduction on that day.

Anticipating the retreat of the enemy, Johnston's division was sent during the night to his rear on the Martinsburg road at Stephens Station, some four or five miles from Winchester. We had hardly gotten to position before the enemy appeared and, discovering their way blocked, made a vigorous effort to cut through our lines; but they were repulsed, and over three thousand surrendered. A small number, including General Milroy and his cavalry, escaped. The entire number of prisoners captured by us was about 4,000, together with a number of pieces of artillery, wagons and stores. The fighting and casualties were not heavy; but withal, the enterprise was well and skilfully managed by the Confederates. If there was a lack of wise leadership on the part of the enemy it was in not retiring in time.

We now moved on toward the Potomac, crossing into Maryland near Shepherdstown about the 20th. The Maryland line, one of the regiments of our brigade of Johnston's division, was given the honor of being at the head of the column, because we were entering their State. Before reaching the river the excellent band of this regiment had gone forward and had taken position in the middle of the stream, a little above the broad and shallow ford, and as the head of the column entered the ford, the melodious strains of "Maryland, My Maryland" floated out from the band with such forceful expression as to stir to the depths the emotions of these war worn veterans of so many fields. The memory of this event when recalled will be of interest doubtless to those who witnessed it.

We moved on to camp near Sharpsburg and near the great battle grounds of less than a year before. Here we remained two or three days. Thence the course of our division was to Greencastle, thence our brigade made a detour to the left to disperse a militia force and to also gather supplies, thence by McConnelsburg to Chambersburg and on toward Carlisle.

We were still west of the Blue Ridge and in the beautiful valley of the Cumberland. Our march was easterly toward Harrisburg, but about the 29th, our direction was suddenly changed to the south toward Gettysburg. We passed through the mountain range into the beautiful Susquehanna valley in which Gettysburg is located, and approached that place from the northeast over the Harrisburg road, reaching position late in the afternoon of July 1st, and after the first day's battle, which had occurred earlier in the day between Heth's and Pender's divisions of A.P. Hill's corps and the First and Eleventh corps of the Federals, resulting in the retirement of the latter in great confusion to Cemetery Hill, already fortified and occupied by another corps of Federals under General Steinwehr. The battle was spirited and sanguinary, resulting in nearly a complete annihilation of the first corps of the Federals and the capture of two pieces of artillery and over two thousand prisoners by the Confederates. This ended the first day's battle just two months after the first day's battle at Chancellorsville; and it was now as then the first day of the month.

The second day of the battle and of the month was to be a day of supreme effort, and the commanders of the two armies hurried their forces to position during the night. The responsibility was upon them and they were supposed to know conditions and advantages and to avail themselves of them. Was this done? Was any advantage of position that might have been taken overlooked, not seen, or seen and lost by either side? This must be decided by military experts from the facts.

At nightfall of the 1st the Federals held Cemetery Hill. On the morning of the 2d they occupied and had fortified that part of their final line, including Culp's Hill on their right, thence south along the ridge, including Cemetery Hill to Little Round Top; and later in the day they extended their left so as to embrace Little and Big Round Tops, and to their right so as to embrace Wolf Hill. This formation was somewhat in the shape of a great hook – Big Round Top, thence to Cemetery Hill, representing the shank, Cemetery, Culp's and Wolf Hills the curve to the point. The Confederate right occupied Seminary Ridge, thence to the left to Oak Ridge, thence with Oak Ridge to the north of the town, thence around the bend of the hook, conforming to the formation of the Federal line. Big and Little Round Tops and Culp's Hill dominated, and Cemetery Hill equaled in strength any part of the Confederate position. Longstreet of the Confederates held the right, Hill the center, and Ewell the left. Of the Federals, the twelfth corps under Slocum was on the right, occupying Culp's Hill. To his left, occupying Cemetery Hill, the first and eleventh corps; to their left, the second corps under General Hancock extended the line to Little Round Top; the third corps under General Sickels occupied a ridge to the front of the Federal left. The fifth and sixth corps were in reserve. The Federals had entrenched their already strong position and assumed the defensive.

The ominous calm before the storm now prevailed until about the middle of the afternoon, at which time Longstreet advanced to the attack of Sickels. The contest was furious and sanguinary from the beginning. The Peach Orchard, Loop, Wheatfield and Devil's Den, so often won and lost, were made historic by reason of the bloody fierceness of the contest. Sickels was reinforced from time to time with fresh troops, thus increasing the extension and fury of the contest until much of the opposing armies were engaged, and so continued until about 5 o'clock, resulting in the Federals being forced from the field and back to their entrenchments on the ridge. After this battle Ewell and Hill moved against the Federal right on Cemetery and Culp's Hills. The contest was ferocious from the beginning, and so continued to its end.

At Cemetery Hill the Confederates under Hays and Hoke, as did their antagonists under Slocum, gained immortal fame. The former fought their way to the summit of the hill, captured the works and many pieces of artillery, "and when the mix-up made guns of little use the men fought with guns as clubs, stones, rammers and even fists." But fresh Federal reinforcements compelled the exhausted Confederates to relinquish this costly capture and retire to their lines.

Simultaneous with the attack on Cemetery Hill, Johnston's division, occupying the Confederate extreme left, moved against Culp's Hill. The advance was across Rock Creek, a small but rugged stream with deep stretches reaching up to the waist, thence through timber and undergrowth up the slope to the steep ascent, thence up to the entrenched Federals. The fire was withering, but did not impede the charge. The part of the works in its front were carried by the "3rd Brigade" and the retreating Federals were pushed back from the works to the west summit of the hill. The battle continued until about 9 o'clock. We occupied this advance position until morning, when we retired to the entrenchments captured in the early part of the night. In the early morning of the 3d, the Federals in heavy force made a furious attack on Johnston's Division, directing its heaviest blows against our position and brigade to regain the entrenchments. After one of the most determined and bloody battles yet fought the attack was repulsed with heavy loss to the Federals. The Confederates now became the aggressors and pursued the Federals along the top of the hill or small mountain. Here the Federals were found to be so well entrenched and with such formidable obstructions in his front that the position was practically unassailable from the front; so an order to retire was given, but not before we had been well paid for our temerity in advancing against this position.

The engagement had continued for several hours with great fury. Before its beginning the first Maryland Regiment of our brigade had in some way learned of the position, in the Federal line in our front, of the first Maryland regiment of the Federal army; and, so it was then reported, sought and was assigned to position in the Confederate line in its front. Here was a contest truly of old friends, acquaintances and in some instances, relatives arrayed against each other. All the courage, manhood and pride in each was aroused and the bloody strife between these two regiments was more desperately furious, if possible, than at other parts of the line; but the Confederates, as stated, prevailed. A beautiful monument has been erected on the spot, in commemoration of the valor of this regiment, which was at the time of my visit, the only Confederate monument of the hundreds erected to the Federals on this vast battlefield, long since owned and beautified by the Government. Its monuments, statues, splendid roads of many miles reaching every point of interest, its observation towers and its well kept grounds are worth the trouble and expense of a pilgrimage to see them. But I have digressed.

We now retired to the entrenchments we had left, but were ordered about noon to a new line three hundred yards to the rear. This change of position was necessary because a strong force now threatened our left and rear. At our new line I was placed in command of the skirmish line which I disposed so as to protect our flank, as well as front. The game of sharpshooting was now open and was well played by both sides. We held this position during the rest of the day.

About noon of that day the most terrific artillery duel of the war, and perhaps of all time, occurred. Malvern Hill and Fredericksburg had been theretofore considered the fields of greatest artillery duels, but they were toyings in comparison. The Federals had 300 guns of various caliber, and the Confederates 190. Nearly four hundred of these guns were engaged for nearly two hours sending forth their missiles of death and destruction. "The air was filled with hissing shot and bursting shell." The detonations of thunder during a great storm could not be compared to the detonations of the artillery in this duel.

At its end came Pickett's world famous charge, which has been so often written of that it needs no detailed recital here. His force was estimated at about 14,000 men. The distance across the smooth open plain between his position on Seminary Ridge and the Federal lines on Cemetery Hill, his objective point of attack, was more than a mile. The artillery duel had moderated to occasional shots at the time of the start, but as soon as the line debouched from the woods, moving at double quick time, the Federal artillery opened upon this long line, stretching across the Federal front for over a mile, with solid shot until half the distance had been traversed, then with shell and later grape, and then cannister, tearing great gaps in the ranks which were quickly closed, and onward the line sped. They now met the infantry fire which decimated their ranks still more rapidly. They did not falter, but pressed forward to a hand-to-hand contest with the foe, capturing a part of his line at the angle and a number of pieces of his artillery.

Victory now appeared to be won and General Armistead, who had lead his brigade, sharing this belief laid his hand upon a piece of the captured artillery and with the other waved his hat aloft on the point of his sword in ecstacy because of the victory, but here fresh relays of Federals began to pour in against the well nigh exhausted Confederates and opened fire. General Armistead and many others were killed, and with no support at hand the Confederates were compelled to retire and again traverse this wide, open plain of death and destruction. Here Meade failed to avail himself of a most important rule in military science by not returning Pickett's charge. Everything was favorable for it and he had two fresh corps at hand. Pickett's ranks were decimated, exhausted and practically without ammunition; and in Lee's center immediately in front a gap of more than a mile – from Hill's right to Longstreet's left – existed. A more favorable opportunity seldom occurs for the sundering in twain and beating in detail the wings of a great army. Had conditions been reversed, Lee would unquestionably have availed himself of such an opportunity.

This practically ended the battle of Gettysburg, and both armies rested on their arms during the night and following day. During the time nothing occurred, except one or two contests between small detachments from the opposing armies and some skirmishing. This great battle fraught with so many probabilities was over. Sixty-eight thousand Confederates had assaulted ninety-seven thousand Federals in entrenched position and on the enemy's own soil, and had failed. The tide of Confederate hopes and prospects had been in the ascendant up to this crushing blow. That blunders lost the victory to the Confederates has seemingly been conceded, but who committed them has been a question of bitter discussion through the press between Longstreet, Fitz Lee, Early and others. Such generally occurs after the loss of a great battle. It is much easier after than before to see what should and should not have been done, but the discussion of this question, however, will not be taken up here.

Recently I went over this field for the first time since the battle.

CHAPTER TWELVE

☆   ☆   ☆   ☆

Strength of the Federal Position. Three Days
Battle. Retired to Hagerstown. Remained
There Eight Days. Return to Virginia.

Lee, as plainly appears, was at great disad-
vantage in respect to position. He held the arc and
his lines were about four miles long, while Meade
held the chord of the arc and his lines were but little
over one mile long. The difference in distances enabled Meade to reach with reinforcements any part
of his lines in less than a third of the time necessary
for Lee. Looking at conditions as then existing there
would seem to be much in the claim that Meade
should have been maneuvered out of this stronghold, and especially so after he had taken Little
Round Top – the key to the field – the possession of
which alone by the Confederates would have rendered the Federal position untenable.

This could have been captured without material opposition had the attack been made against the

Federal left at dawn on the 2d, instead of at 2 p.m. One hour earlier than 2 would have sufficed for this important capture. At about 3 o'clock Hood, with Benning's and Anderson's brigades, flanked the Federal left and fought his way to it and ascended its rugged, western side; but Vincent's Federal brigade had reached its summit just in time to meet the assault, and being rapidly reinforced held the position. Delay lost it. This gained would have won the battle for the Confederates.

During Longstreet's fight, in which he met relay after relay of fresh troops and accomplished many brilliant feats, driving back in the end the Federals to their final line on the ridge, the corps of Ewell and Hill, facing the Federal right, stood by without firing a gun. This left Meade free to hurl his fresh reserves against Longstreet and beat him to exhaustion. Then Ewell and Hill moved against the Federal right at Culp's and Cemetery Hills, Meade again being left free to concentrate his reinforcements against them. The fight at Culp's Hill continued until about noon of the 3d. After this Pickett's division, being the only fresh Confederates, made the famous charge already mentioned. Thus the great "Army of Northern Virginia" had been beaten in detail. The concentration of the Federals by reason of position gave them the advantage, while distance prevented Lee from reinforcing his wings in time. Then, too, there was lack of simultaneous advance and cooperation; time and distance prevented the necessary quick communication and movement of troops. It is difficult, if not impossible, for large, separate bodies of troops to move at the same time from the circumference to a central point, as was necessary here.

Looking back it is quite plausible that the best hope was in an attack at dawn against Meade's left, which at that time could have been easily turned and his position won, as it would have threatened his rear and communications with Washington, and would also have protected Lee's communications as well.

This battle and campaign was the crucial period of the Confederacy. It was an open secret, gained from rumor, that success would bring recognition of her independence by England, and later by France. Other nations would doubtless fall in line, and the blockade of her ports would soon have been raised. Credit and trade relations with other nations, the enlargement of her armies and munitions of war, would follow; and permanent independence would be established. The high tide of Confederate hopes and prospects were now passed, and on the night of the 4th Lee retired toward Hagerstown. His army was much weakened and in great need of rest. The Federals made one or two feeble attacks on our rear guard which were promptly repulsed.

On the afternoon of the 5th I was placed in command of a detail of men and wagons and directed to make a detour to the left of the column to gather food supplies. I was provided with Confederate currency with which to pay for such supplies. My route was over a mile out and parallel with the course of the column. The well supplied homes enabled me to soon load the wagons and get them under way on a country road that converged toward the column. I now discovered a battalion of Federal cavalry in the distance, bearing down upon us. I ordered the teamsters to move forward with all speed. We quickly reached the outer edge of the open lands and entered the thickly wooded course of the narrow road, so closely pursued that I was compelled to give battle.

I had time to place my men and deliver fire at close range with signal effect on men and horses. This sudden, and perhaps unexpected attack, threw them into great confusion, necessitating a reformation further back. They had, however, discovered the inadequacy of my force and were rapidly reforming. I saw the wagons some distance to my front, curving to the right, the road evidently entering the little valley to my right about three hundred yards to the front. The valley thus formed the chord of the circle, and hence was shorter than the road which formed the circle, but my advanced position gave advantage in distance. I now started with all possible speed with my little force toward this junction of road and valley, and almost immediately the charge up the valley began as anticipated. It was an exciting struggle. My men were strung out quite a distance along the way; and as we neared the junction, the race was about even, with forces moving on parallel lines a short distance apart. My men now opened fire and luckily shot some of the foremost horses just as they were entering a narrow pass in their front. This blocked the way, impeded the charge and threw the cavalry into confusion which was increased by the continual firing of my command. Farther on we took an advantageous position, but were soon relieved by Confederate cavalry and rejoined the passing column.

The column reached the vicinity of Hagerstown on the evening of the 6th. The Potomac River by reason of recent rains was much swollen and intervened between Lee's army and Virginia from whence ammunition, now practically exhausted, had to be procured. The army was placed in position and entrenched itself against the approaching Federal army which did not appear in its front until the 12th but failed to attack or to show an intention of so doing. Tired of waiting longer, Lee withdrew his army on the early morning of the 15th to Virginia. Ewell's Corps now remained in the valley for some time, then moved to the east side of the Blue Ridge. Nothing of importance transpired with this corps during the remaining season. On the approach of winter, camp was pitched in Orange county in rear of the Rapidan River. Thus ended the campaigns of 1863.

Point Lookout Prison Camp, Maryland

CHAPTER THIRTEEN

☆ ☆ ☆ ☆

Wilderness Campaign. Fighting on Way to
Spottsylvania Court House. Capture of
Part of Johnson's Division. Prison Life.
War Ends. Return Home.

About the first days of May, 1864, our division (Johnston's) struck camp and moved on the old Orange and Fredericksburg turnpike toward Germainia Ford of the Rapidan to meet the advancing Federals, and thus the great wilderness campaign began. About noon of the 5th, the advance brigade of Ewell's column met and engaged the Federals, who had already crossed the river. During this engagement at the front, the corps was formed in the rear, and in a brief space of time threw up slight works for protection. The Federals moved forward and made several light attacks upon our position, which were repulsed. The enemy placed and used to our annoyance a battery well supported within six or seven hundred yards of our position. Upon this our brigade, together with Battle's, charged near night and captured it. During the night our fortifications were very much strengthened. On the 6th heavy skirmishing continued at intervals until late in the afternoon, at which time a part of the left of Ewell's corps made an attack on the Federal right, capturing his works and driving him back more than a mile, capturing several hundred prisoners, including Brigadier Generals Seymour and Shaler. Nothing of importance occurred on the 7th, except occasional skirmishing. On the 8th, we moved toward Spottsylvania Court House. It was a trying march because of the intense heat, dust and smoke from burning woods. Here late in the afternoon we found the Confederate cavalry engaged in battle with Federal infantry. Our lines were quickly formed and by the morning of the 8th well entrenched.

Johnston's division occupied a position in the front line, some distance to the right of an angle in the line formed by the extension of the line around the end of a ridge. This projecting ridge was an ideal position for artillery, commanding the open plain in front, and on the sides of the angle as well. The importance of the position had been recognized and a number of pieces of artillery were well placed upon it and protected by suitable works, as well as by the fortified line of battle which extended around this point in front and below these guns, thus making the position quite strong. The continuation of the line to the left curved farther in, presenting its convex front to the Federal lines and enabling the reserves from their positions in the concave space between the wings to speedily reinforce any part of the line as occasion might require. Our skirmish line was well to the front, and heavy skirmishing occurred during the day; but the night was quiet, giving opportunity for sleep and rest so much needed.

On the 10th skirmishing and artillery fire at intervals was kept up during the day until late in the afternoon, when the Federals made a heavy attack on that part of the Confederate lines held by the brigades of Doles and Daniel, capturing the fortifications, several hundred prisoners, a number of pieces of artillery, and driving the Confederates some distance to the rear.

Reinforcements, of which our brigade formed a part, were hurried across the field to restore the broken lines. We soon met the now victorious Federals in open field, and the fight was furious from the beginning. A charge was ordered, and we swept them back over the works, capturing a number of prisoners and recapturing the artillery. The loss of both sides was heavy. The lines being restored, our brigades were ordered to their former positions and there rested on their arms for the night.

On the 11th, nothing of importance occurred, except an all day downpour of rain. Not even the opposing picket lines disturbed each other. Near nightfall, however, the Confederate artillery was removed from the ridge above mentioned to the rear. It was a matter of comment at the time as to what it meant; men wondered if it was the beginning of a withdrawal.

Furthermore, a detail for skirmish duty was taken from the line at the angle, thus weakening it to that extent. And so passed this wet and mirky night of the 11th. Details had also been sent back to prepare and bring rations to the men who slept upon their arms.

At dawn of the 12th, firing on the skirmish line began and was soon general along our entire front. We knew it meant a general attack. I was now in command of the regiment by reason of seniority of rank, and hence rushed along the line to see that the men were up and in position. By this time the skirmish line had gotten in and reported a general advance in heavy force. The ground in our front was rolling and the advancing column could not be seen until within a hundred and fifty yards. They began to come into view as they ascended the gentle rise, coming to full view at a distance of a hundred yards. The first line advanced in splendid order, as if on dress parade; close in their rear was a supporting line, advancing with confident tread, and when within a hundred yards or less, the first volley of our line was opened upon them with frightful effect, which at once caused a pause and swaying of the line. A continuance of the fire now caused a precipitate retreat onto the supporting line, causing great confusion in their ranks. The continued, rapid fire, put the entire force to hasty retreat; but almost immediately new lines took up the advance, met the same reception, and were repulsed as were their predecessors. At this time large numbers of Federals were crossing our works at the angle referred to, and the Confederates were giving back rapidly. This heavy force passed down a deep ravine to our left rear and charged upon us. Hence I ordered the rear rank to fire to the rear and the front rank to the front. This had but little effect, however, as their numbers were so overwhelming.

I had sent twice to my brigade commander for permission to throw the left of my regiment back, and thus be in position to continue the fight – or to retire if circumstances should so require; – but he commanded me to hold my position, saying that Gorden would come to our aid in due time. The position had been held by Johnston's division in the hope of assistance until too late to escape capture by the overwhelming force in rear, as well as in front; and thus a large part of this division of men and officers, including Generals Johnston and Stuart, was captured, as were a number of pieces of artillery which had arrived on the field too late for use, but in due time for capture. This inexcusable blunder and its results was a severe blow to Lee's army, not only because of the loss of men and guns, but because of the moral effect. All of which would not have occurred if the artillery had not been withdrawn from this vital part of the line, so strong and easy to be held when properly manned.

During the engagement I noticed the regimental flagpole inverted and a white handkerchief displayed at its top. I quickly caught it and again hoisted the flag, and held it while the men were being forced to surrender along the line on each side of the position we occupied. A small number rallied around me and for some time fought without other hope than that the reserves might come to our aid. The Federals now charged against our front and rear, bringing injury and death to some of our little band around the colors.

I was still holding the flag and had not surrendered. The Federals were around us. Louis Fitch, a private soldier of my own company, and the others were by my side. Fitch discovered a Federal soldier bearing down upon us and immediately fired upon him. The momentum of this soldier carried him forward as he fell and his bayonet well aimed penetrated the ground at my feet, and at the moment I heard the blow of a sword made by a Federal lieutenant against the barrel of a gun, and in my glance at the instant I saw the bayoneted gun being forced to the ground. I have regretted my failure to get the name of this lieutenant, confusion and hurry of all at the time prevented. As to Fitch, there was no better soldier in the army than he. In camp, on the march and in battle he was the same. In the thickest of the fight his clarion voice which cheered and inspired his comrades could be heard above the din and roar of battle.

But I have digressed from my purpose to specialize none from the many who were so worthy; but the digression in this instance I am sure will be excused.

All were now overpowered and rushed to the rear of the Federal lines. Ten minutes after, perhaps – but too late to save this splendid division and munitions – our reserves opened fire on this flanking

army and kept up a bloody battle during the day.
Hence the name in history, "Bloody Angle." So near
were we at its beginning that some of our men were
wounded by Confederate balls. We were now gradually brought together as all were hurried farther to
the rear.

I came up with Generals Johnston and Stuart,
both of whom I knew well. In discussing the disaster
they both attributed it to the unaccountable absence
of the artillery from its strong and vital position. We
were now approaching General Hancock mounted,
booted and spurred. His superb bearing and strength
of personality indicated the born soldier. As soon as
he recognized Johnston and Stuart, his late comrades
in the Federal army, he spurred his charger to them
and gave them a cordial greeting, after which he
called a major of his staff and directed him to take
them to his headquarters and see that every comfort
be given them. He bade them the time of day, jestingly stating he would see them later, but must look
after a little business farther on, and at once went
rapidly toward the front, where the battle was raging
fiercer than before. We now lost sight of Johnston
and Stuart and passed on through a large army, to
say nothing of those engaged at the front. Its numbers, its vast artillery, munitions and general equipment could but impress us with the disadvantages
the Confederates labored under from these unequal
conditions. About three miles to the rear we were
halted in an open field, and surrounded by a force of
infantry and a number of pieces of artillery bearing

upon us. Here the officers were separated from the men. The ground here occupied by us was low, flat, exceedingly wet and soft, as a result of the rain of the day before. We had no resting place save the wet and muddy ground, and could do nothing to gain rest but move about in our limited space, which was soon converted into a thin mud of two or three inches in depth.

Here we remained during that day and night, on our feet or sitting or lying in the mud, until the following morning, without food save a small piece of raw beef issued at about 10 o'clock at night to each of the hungry men who, perforce, ate it raw. Most of us had not had food for more than two days, and were nearly exhausted from the strenuous duties before and hardships after capture. About midnight I was fortunate enough to find a piece of fence rail about four feet long which served as my bed, and thus kept my body out of the mud; and, notwithstanding there was tramping around and perhaps over me during the night, I slept soundly until morning. A few others may have found similar beds, but those not so fortunate either tramped all night or slept in a bed of mud.

The morning of the 13th opened bright, and better rations were issued to us. We were moved toward the Potomac at Acquia Creek by way of Fredericksburg and the Rappahannock. The day was hot and the march fatiguing. We reached the Potomac and were again placed in low open ground and surrounded by soldiers and artillery. On the following morning we were placed aboard a transport and moved down the Potomac – accompanied by two gunboats – to Point Lookout, Maryland, a narrow point of sand jutting out between Chesapeake Bay and the Atlantic Ocean. Here we remained in tents until the first days of June, when on a hot afternoon the entire camp of about four hundred officers were taken on the lower deck of a cattle transport for removal to Fort Delaware. The space was crowded and we lacked sanitary conveniences and proper ventilation. The excessive heat, increased by the heat of the vessel's engine which occupied the middle of the space, made conditions so desperate as to almost produce serious scrambles for air and existence. One died and a number were prostrated, A heavy guard occupied the top deck and allowed fifteen of our number to go on this deck for air and life for fifteen minutes, and then fifteen others to take their places. We at once lined up, so that every one should in turn enjoy this privilege.

The transport stood out in the Bay for the night with two men-of-war standing by as additional guards. After the cool sea breezes died down at about 8 p.m., the sense of suffocation was hardly endurable. The long, sleepless hours of the night finally passed, and at early morning the transport and men-of-war started for Fort Delaware, situated on a small island in Delaware Bay at the mouth of Delaware River. We reached the fort in the afternoon of the same day, and were assigned to quarters in the thirty-three board structures, already partially occupied by previous prisoners of war.

These structures, called divisions, occupied three sides of a square, and each accommodated about a hundred and twenty-five persons. Tiers of three shelves seven feet wide served for sleeping quarters in these structures, which had small diamond shaped openings in the outer wall to serve for observation by sentinels. The duty of keeping in order these divisions devolved on the inmates, performed by daily details. Entertainments were such as the varied talents of our numbers could devise. Of these Divine service, debates, readings, and theatricals occupied greatest attention. Marked talent in all these lines was in great abundance. The absolute necessity for some principle or question of general interest strong enough to engage and hold attention and require mental and physical effort to accomplish that something, was apparent.

In this view practical politics was found to be the most engaging. This was developed and made manifest by the organization of a government among ourselves on the lines of our State governments. The elective offices were nearly or quite as bitterly contested for by rival aspirants and parties as in the States.

Discussion of principles and policies gave general entertainment, and hence distracted attention from prison and prison life. After a very hot contest in my own division I was honored by election to a seat in the general assembly, and enjoyed the service very much.

Many questions of profound interest were discussed with great ability. Of amusements the weekly theatricals attracted much attention. The wisdom, wit, humor and burlesque of the bright and well-equipped troupe were apt and catchy. A very amusing but valuable episode occurred at one of these performances. Friends within Federal lines had sent at various times by express to prison friends boxes of stationery and clothing. Some of these boxes had been rifled of their most valuable contents. Complaint had been unavailing.

The Commander of the district was on a visit of inspection to the Commander of the post and they, with a number of officers of lower grade, on invitation attended a performance. The house was well filled. Witticisms and hits soon put all in good humor. This was heightened by the culminating scene designated "Card Scene." Half a dozen emaciated, careworn, poorly clad Confederates seated on the floor were intensely engaged in a game of cards. The contest was earnest and the acting of the participants was good and true to nature. In the midst of the game, a Federal sergeant in fatigue uniform appeared on a parapet wall, as was done in the daily routine outside, and announced "box call." Cards were dropped and a rush was made to the wall. Boxes were called and brought on the stage for three of the number, who proceeded with much eagerness and joy to open in succession the boxes.

While thus engaged each recounted the contents of which the sweetheart of one, the mother of another and the friend of the other had apprised them by letter. Much needed suits of clothing, shoes, stationary and other articles were enumerated. The manifested ecstacy of the actors in anticipation of these stores was very amusing, but the first articles revealed were a tattered and faded blue fatigue jacket and trousers, instead of the new suit. Then old rusty and worn shoes and other articles. These old articles had been substituted for nearly all the new ones. The comments of surprise by the actors as to why the sweetheart and why the mother had perpetrated such cruel jokes on them were shrewd and pointed and so adroitly presented the grievance that the Federal officers enjoyed it very much, and declared the entertainment to be one of the most enjoyable they had ever witnessed. This ended the evil complained of.

A pathetic incident occurred later. A young soldier of fine physique decided to make application for release from prison on his oath of allegiance to the United States government. He was of my own company, a splendid soldier and seemingly of perpetual buoyant spirits. He was taken to the probationary – commonly called galvanized barracks. There with strangers he soon repented his course and applied and was granted permission to return to his comrades, whose barracks adjoined but were separated by a high wall from that of the officers.

His comrades ignored him. The comradeship he had always enjoyed was no longer his. The strain was too great. He grew despondent and sick at heart.

His declining condition was rapid and quite apparent to all. He was sent to the hospital, of which happenings I was kept informed by letters from some of the men wrapped about a small stone and thrown to the officers' grounds. I went to the hospital at once and found this man in a precarious condition. I interviewed his attending surgeon, who told me the man was physically sound in every respect, and that his trouble was mental. In consequence of which his nerve force was near to complete collapse; that the occurrences above mentioned which I had related to the surgeon were the cause of it. He was deeply interested in the case and assured me he would do all he could to save this worthy man. My leave was now out and I returned to barracks for the night. On the following morning, on permission, I hastened to the hospital; and on arrival found that this soldier, recognized as of the best, who had borne himself as such on many hard fought fields, had of a broken heart passed over the river to the other shore. Peace to his ashes.

Prison fare and treatment, so far as I have been able to form an opinion based on experience and on written accounts, were much the same in Federal and Confederate prisons. Ill treatment and even cruelties occurred in both – not, as I believe, by sanction or tolerance of governmental authority, but by malignant individual soldiers or persons in petty authority. I will not, however, at this late day go into details, thinking it better to throw the mantle of charity over the subject and let it be forgotten.

I began the study of my profession of law and pursued it during my thirteen months of prison life and completed the course after my liberation. This was not only a delightful entertainment, but was in the line of equipment for my work in life. I have never regretted this course, but on the contrary have enjoyed the profession and its associations in which I have had a satisfactory measure of success.

At the time of my capture I little thought that my service in the field was ended. But on the contrary I expected to be exchanged very soon and return to my command; but at this time the Federal authorities ceased to grant further exchanges of prisoners, it being easier to deplete Confederate ranks by holding prisoners than to exchange and meet them and deplete their ranks on the field. Hence prisoners were held until after the close of the war in April, 1865. Our prison gates were thrown open on June 13, 1865, and prisoners returned thence to their respective homes.

Thus ended my career as a soldier. I now returned to my father and mother, brothers and sisters at the old homestead, near Gate City in Scott county, Virginia. The comfortable but old-fashioned home, its porches, broad stone steps, the negro cabins, the public highway in front, the babbling brook farther on that flows through the valley, the great mountain standing still farther to the front, were always before, but now in the month of June doubly dear to me, and while yet but little more than a boy, although disappointed in the results of the war, I was made to feel that life was still worth the living.

Many changes had taken place. The well tilled fields and green pastures were not luxuriant as before, lowing cattle, the colts and their dams, the music and dancing of the younger negroes, were missing – but only the older negroes still remained.

The ravages of war had wrought the great change. I now turned my attention for the time being to the harvest field and the farm, no longer a soldier, but a citizen.

The war was over and the people of the South accepted its results in honesty and good-faith. They had made a brave, manly and determined battle for the right as they saw it, but had been defeated by numbers and equipment. Honor, dignity, and self-respect they still had. They were not rebels as they had not rebelled against lawful authority, but fought for a right as they and their ancestors viewed it, that was denied them. They had been taught from the beginning that when England was trying to subject the colonies, each of which was sovereign, a compact was formed by these colonies as States for mutual aid and defense. Each expressly reserved its sovereignty not expressly delegated; hence it was claimed that the Constitution did not set up a national government above and over the States, but was simply a compact between independent and sovereign States, each having the right to resume its sovereignty at will. Thus schooled and so understanding their rights the people of the South felt justified in their course, and their integrity of purpose cannot be questioned; but when these questions were settled by the arbitrament of the sword, they returned to citizenship and the building up of their waste places – and with the same integrity of purpose have been loyal to the flag of our country, and today there is no section of the Union in which there is more American blood and American patriotism than in the late Confederate States. But few if any would now change the result.

APPENDIX

Stonewall Jackson's Last Battle
by James Power Smith
Aide-de-camp to Lt.-Gen. T. J. Jackson

At daybreak on the morning of the 29th of April, 1863, sleeping in our tents at corps headquarters, near Hamilton's Crossing, we were aroused by Major Samuel Hale, of Early's staff; with the stirring news that Federal troops were crossing the Rappahannock on pontoons under cover of a heavy fog. General Jackson had spent the night at Mr. Yerby's hospitable mansion near by, where Mrs. Jackson had brought her infant child for the father to see. He was at once informed, and promptly issued to his division commanders orders of preparation for action. At his direction I rode a mile across the fields to army headquarters, and finding General Robert E. Lee still slumbering quietly, at the suggestion of Colonel Venable, whom I found stirring, I entered his tent and awoke the general. Turning his feet out of his cot he sat upon its side as I gave him the tidings from the front. Expressing no surprise, he playfully said: "Well, I thought I heard firing, and was beginning to think it was time some of you young fellows were coming to tell me what it was all about. Tell your good general that I am sure he knows what to do. I will meet him at the front very soon."

It was Sedgwick who had crossed, and, marching along the river front to impress us with his numbers, was now intrenching his line on the river road, under cover of Federal batteries on the north bank.

All day long we lay in the old lines of the action of December preceding, watching the operation of the enemy. Nor did we move through the next day, the 30th of April. General Lee had been informed promptly by General J.E.B. Stuart, of the Confederate cavalry, of the movement in force by General Hooker across the Rappahannock upon Chancellorsville; and during the night of Thursday, April 30th, General Jackson withdrew his corps, leaving Early and his division with Barksdale's brigade to hold the old lines from Hamilton's Crossing along the rear of Fredericksburg.

By the light of a brilliant moon, at midnight, that passed into an early dawn of dense mist, the troops were moved, by the Old Mine road, out of sight of the enemy, until, about eleven a.m. of Friday, May 1st, they reached Anderson's position, confronting Hooker's advance from Chancellorsville, near the Tabernacle Church on the plank road.

To meet the whole Army of the Potomac, under Hooker, General Lee had of all arms about sixty thousand men. General Longstreet, with part of his corps, was absent below Petersburg. General Lee had two divisions of Longstreet's corps, Anderson's and McLaws's, and Jackson's corps, consisting of four divisions, A. P. Hill's, D. H. Hill's commanded by Rodes, Trimble's commanded by Colston, and Early's; and about a hundred and seventy pieces of field artillery. The divisions of Anderson and McLaws had been sent from Fredericksburg to meet Hooker's advance from Chancellorsville; Anderson on Wednesday, and McLaws (except Barksdale's brigade left with Early) on Thursday. At the Tabernacle Church, about four miles east of Chancellorsville, the opposing forces met and brisk skirmishing began. On Friday Jackson, reaching Anderson's position, took command of the Confederate advance, and urged on his skirmish line under Brigadier-General Ramseur with great vigor. How the muskets rattled along a front of a mile or two, across the unfenced fields, and through the woodlands! What spirit was imparted to the line, and cheers rolled along its length, when Jackson, and then Lee himself, appeared riding abreast of the line along the plank road! Slowly but steadily the line advanced, until at nightfall all Federal pickets and skirmishers were driven back upon the body of Hooker's force at Chancellorsville.

Here we reached a point, a mile and a half from Hooker's lines, where a road turns down to the left toward the old Catherine Furnace; and here at the fork of the roads General Lee and General Jackson spent the night, resting on the pine straw, curtained only by the close shadow of the pine forest. A little after night-fall, I was sent by General Lee upon an errand to General A. P. Hill, on the old stone turnpike a mile or two north; and returning some time later with information of matters on our right, I found General Jackson retired to rest, and General Lee sleeping at the foot of a tree, covered with his army cloak. As I aroused the sleeper, he slowly sat up on the ground and said, "Ah, Captain, you have returned, have you? Come here and tell me what you have learned on the right." Laying his hand on me he drew me down by his side, and, passing his arm around my shoulder, drew me near to him in a fatherly way that told of his warm and kindly heart. When I had related such information as I had secured for him, he thanked me for accomplishing his commission, and then said he regretted that the young men about General Jackson had not relieved him of annoyance, by finding a battery of the enemy which had harassed our advance, adding that the young men of that day were not equal to what they were when he was a young man. Seeing immediately that he was jesting and disposed to rally me, as he often did young officers, I broke away from the hold on me which he tried to retain, and, as he laughed heartily through the stillness of the night, I went off to make a bed of my saddle-blanket, and, with my head in my saddle, near my horse's feet, was soon wrapped in the heavy slumber of a wearied soldier.

Some time after midnight I was awakened by the chill of the early morning hours, and, turning over, caught a glimpse of a little flame on the slope above me, and sitting up to see what it meant I saw, bending over a scant fire of twigs, two men seated on old cracker boxes and warming their hands over the little fire. I had but to rub my eyes and collect my wits to recognize the figures of Robert E. Lee and Stonewall Jackson. Who can tell the story of that quiet council of war between two sleeping armies? Nothing remains on record to tell of plans discussed, and dangers weighed, and a great purpose formed, but the story of the great day so soon to follow.

It was broad daylight, and the thick beams of yellow sunlight came through the pine branches, when some one touched me rudely with his foot, saying, "Get up, Smith, the general wants you!" As I leaped to my feet, the rhythmic click of the canteens of marching infantry caught my ear. Already in motion! What could it mean? In a moment I was mounted and at the side of the general, who sat on his horse by the roadside, as the long line of our troops cheerily, but in silence as directed, poured down the Furnace road. His cap was pulled low over his eyes, and, looking up from under the visor, with lips compressed, indicating the firm purpose within, he nodded to me, and in brief and rapid utterance, without a superfluous word, as though all were distinctly formed in his mind and beyond question, he gave me orders for our wagon and ambulance trains. From the open fields in our rear, at the head of the

Catharpin road, all trains were to be moved upon that road to Todd's tavern, and thence west by interior roads, so that our troops would be between them and the enemy at Chancellorsville.

My orders delivered and the trains set in motion, I returned to the site of our night's bivouac, to find that General Jackson and staff had followed the marching column.

Who was the young ordnance officer who so kindly fed my horse at the tail of his wagon and then added the few camp biscuits which were breakfast, dinner, and supper to me that day? Many thanks to my unknown friend.

Slow and tedious is the advance of a mounted officer who has to pass in narrow wood roads through dense thickets, the packed column of marching infantry, to be recognized all along the line and good-naturedly chaffed by many a gay-spirited fellow: "Say, here's one of Old Jack's little boys; let him by, boys!" in a most patronizing tone. "Have a good breakfast this morning, sonny?" "Better hurry up, or you'll catch it for getting behind." "Tell Old Jack we're all a-comm'." "Don't let him begin the fuss till we get thar!" And so on, until about three p.m., after a ride of ten miles of tortuous road, I found the general, seated on a stump by the Brock road, writing this dispatch:

Near 3 p.m., May 2nd, 1863.
General: The enemy has made a stand at Chancellor's, which is about two miles from Chan-

cellorsville. I hope so soon as practicable to attack.

I trust that an ever kind Providence will bless us with success.

Respectfully,

T. J. Jackson,

Lieutenant-General.

General Robert E. Lee.

P. S. The leading division is up, and the next two appear to be well closed.   T.J.J.

The place here mentioned as Chancellor's was also known as Dowdall's Tavern. It was the farm of the Rev. Melzi Chancellor, two miles west of Chancellorsville, and the Federal force found here and at Talley's, a mile farther west, was the Eleventh Corps, under General Howard. General Fitz Lee, with cavalry scouts, had advanced until he had view of the position of Howard's corps, and found them unprotected by pickets, and unsuspicious of a possible attack.

Reaching the Orange plank road, General Jackson himself rode with Fitz Lee to reconnoiter the position of Howard, and then sent the Stonewall brigade of Virginia troops, under Brigadier-General Paxton, to hold the point where the Germanna plank road obliquely enters the Orange road. Leading the main column of his force farther on the Brock road to the old turnpike, the head of the column turned sharply eastward toward Chancellorsville. About a mile had been passed, when he halted and began the disposition of his forces to attack Howard.

Rodes's division, at the head of the column, was thrown into line of battle, with Colston forming the second line and A.P. Hill's the third, while the artillery under Colonel Stapleton Crutchfield moved in column on the road, or was parked in a field on the right. The well-trained skirmishers of Rodes's division, under Major Eugene Blackford, were thrown to the front. It must have been between five and six o'clock in the evening, Saturday, May 2d, when these dispositions were completed. Upon his stout-built, long-paced little sorrel, General Jackson sat, with visor low over his eyes, and lips compressed, and with his watch in his hand. Upon his right sat General Robert E. Rodes, the very picture of a soldier, and every inch all that he appeared. Upon his right sat Major Blackford.

"Are you ready, General, Rodes?" said Jackson.

"Yes, sir!" said Rodes, impatient for the advance.

"You can go forward then," said Jackson.

A nod from Rodes was order enough for Blackford, and then suddenly the woods rang with the bugle call, and back came the responses from bugles on the right and left, and the long line of skirmishers, through the wild thicket of undergrowth, sprang eagerly to their work, followed promptly by the quick steps of the line of battle. For a moment all the troops seemed buried in the depths of the gloomy forest, and then suddenly the echoes waked and swept the country for miles, never failing until heard at the headquarters of Hooker at Chancellors-ville – the wild "rebel yell" of the long Confederate lines.

Never was assault delivered with grander en-thusiasm. Fresh from the long winter's waiting, and confident from the preparation of the spring, the troops were in fine condition and in high spirits. The boys were all back from home or sick leave. "Old Jack" was there upon the road in their midst; there could be no mistake and no failure. And there were Rodes and A.P. Hill. Had they not seen and cheered as long and as loud as they were permitted the gay-hearted Stuart and the splendid Fitz Lee, with long beard and fiery charger? Was not Crutchfield's array of brass and iron "dogs of war" at hand, with Poague and Palmer, and all the rest, ready to bark loud and deep with half a chance?

Alas! for Howard and his unformed lines, and his brigades with guns stacked, and officers at din-ner or asleep under the trees, and butchers deep in the blood of beeves! Scattered through field and for-est, his men were preparing their evening meal. A little show of earthwork facing the south was quick-ly taken by us in reverse from the west. Flying bat-talions are not flying buttresses for an army's stabil-ity. Across Talley's fields the rout begins. Over at Hawkins's hill, on the north of the road, Carl Schurz makes a stand, soon to be driven into the same hope-less panic. By the quiet Wilderness Church in the vale, leaving wounded and dead everywhere, by Melzi Chancellor's, on into the deep thicket again, the Confederate lines press forward, – now broken and all disaligned by the density of bush that tears the clothes away; now halting to load and deliver a volley upon some regiment or fragment of the enemy that will not move as fast as others. Thus the attack upon Hooker's flank was a grand success, beyond the most sanguine expectation.

The writer of this narrative, an aide-de-camp of Jackson's, was ordered to remain at the point where the advance began, to be a center of communication between the general and the cavalry on the flanks, and to deliver orders to detachments of artillery still moving up from the rear.

Whose fine black charger, with such elegant trappings, was that, deserted by his owner and found tied to a tree, which became mine only for that short and eventful nightfall?

It was about eight p.m., in the twilight, that, so comfortably mounted, I gathered my couriers about me and went forward to find General Jackson. The storm of battle had swept far on to the east, and become more and more faint to the ear, until silence came with night over the fields and woods. As I rode along that old turnpike, passing scattered fragments of Confederates looking for their regiments, parties of prisoners concentrating under guards, wounded men by the roadside and under the trees at Talley's and Chancellor's, I had reached an open field on the right, a mile west of Chancellorsville, when, in the dusky twilight, I saw horsemen near an old cabin in the field. Turning toward them, I found

Rodes and his staff engaged in gathering the broken and scattered troops that had swept the two miles of battle-field. "General Jackson is just ahead on the road, Captain," said Rodes; "tell him I will be here at this cabin if I am wanted." I had not gone a hundred yards before I heard firing, a shot or two, and then a company volley upon the right of the road, and another upon the left. A few moments farther on I met Captain Murray Taylor, an aide of A. P. Hill's, with tidings that Jackson and Hill were wounded, and some around them killed, by the fire of their own men. Spurring my horse into a sweeping gallop, I soon passed the Confederate line of battle some three or four rods on its front, found the general's horse beside a pine sapling on the left, and a rod beyond a little party of men caring for a wounded officer. The story of the sad event is briefly told, and very much in essentials as it came to me from the lips of the wounded general himself, and in everything confirmed and completed by those who were eye-witnesses and near companions.

When Jackson had reached the point where his line now crossed the turnpike, scarcely a mile west of Chancellorsville, and not half a mile from a line of Federal troops, he had found his front line unfit for the farther and vigorous advance he desired, by reason of the irregular character of the fighting, now right, now left, and because of the dense thickets, through which it was impossible to preserve alignment. Division commanders found it more and more difficult as the twilight deepened to hold their broken brigades in hand. Regretting the necessity of relieving the troops in front, General Jackson had ordered A. P. Hill's division, his third and reserve line, to be placed in front. While this change was being effected, impatient and anxious, the general rode forward on the turnpike, followed by two or three of his staff and a number of couriers and signal-sergeants. He passed the swampy depression and began the ascent of the hill toward Chancellorsville, when he came upon a line of the Federal infantry lying on their arms. Fired at by one or two muskets (two musket balls from the enemy whistled over my head as I came to the front), he turned and came back toward his line, upon the side of the road to his left. As he rode near to the Confederate troops just placed in position, and ignorant that he was in the front, the left company began firing to the front, and two of his party fell from their saddles dead – Capt. Boswell of the Engineers, and Sergeant Cunliffe of the Signal Corps. Spurring his horse across the road to his right, he was met by a second volley from the right company of Pender's North Carolina Brigade. Under this volley, when not two rods from the troops, the general received three balls at the same instant. One penetrated the palm of his right hand and was cut out that night from the back of his hand. A second passed around the wrist of the left arm and out through the left hand. But a third ball passed through the left arm halfway from shoulder to elbow.

The large bone of the upper arm was splintered to the elbow-joint, and the wound bled freely. His horse turned quickly from the fire, through the thick bushes, which swept the cap from the general's head, and scratched his forehead, leaving drops of blood to stain his face. As he lost his hold upon the bridle-rein, he reeled from the saddle, and was caught by the arms of Captain Milboume of the Signal Corps. Laid upon the ground, there came at once to his succor, General A.P. Hill and members of his staff. The writer reached his side a minute after, to find General Hill holding the head and shoulders of the wounded chief. Cutting open the coat sleeve from wrist to shoulder, I found the wound in the upper arm, and with my handkerchief I bound the arm above the wound to stem the flow of blood. Couriers were sent for Dr. Hunter McGuire, the surgeon of the corps and the general's trusted friend, and for an ambulance.

Being outside of our lines, it was urgent that he should be moved at once. With difficulty litter-bearers were brought from the line near by, the general placed upon the litter, and carefully raised to the shoulder, I myself bearing one corner. A moment after, artillery from the Federal side was opened upon us; great broadsides thundered over the woods; hissing shells searched the dark thickets through, and shrapnels swept the road along which we moved. Two or three steps farther, and the litter-bearer at my side was struck and fell, but, as the litter turned, Major Watkins Leigh, of Hill's staff, happily caught it. But the fright of the men was so great that we were obliged to lay the litter and its burden down upon the road. As the litter-bearers ran to the cover of the trees, I threw myself by the general's side. and held him firmly to the ground as he attempted to rise. Over us swept the rapid fire of shot and shell – grape-shot striking fire upon the flinty rock of the road all around us, and sweeping from their feet horses and men of the artillery just moved to the front. Soon the firing veered to the other side of the road, and I sprang to my feet, assisted the general to rise, passed my arm around him, and with the wounded man's weight thrown heavily upon me, we forsook the road. Entering the woods, he sank to the ground from exhaustion, but the litter was soon brought, and again rallying a few men, we essayed to carry him farther, when a second bearer fell at my side. This time, with none to assist, the litter careened, and the general fell to the ground, with a groan of deep pain. Greatly alarmed, I sprang to his head, and, lifting his head as a stray beam of moonlight came through clouds and leaves, he opened his eyes and wearily said, "Never mind me, Captain, never mind me." Raising him again to his feet, he was accosted by Brigadier-General Pender: "Oh, General, I hope you are not seriously wounded. I will have to retire my troops to re-form them; they are so much broken by this fire." But Jackson, rallying his strength, with firm voice said, "You must hold your ground, General Pender; you must hold your ground, sir!" and so uttered his last command on the field.

Again we resorted to the litter, and with difficulty bore it through the bush, and then under hot and angry fire along the road. Soon an ambulance was reached, and stopping to seek some stimulant at Chancellor's (Dowdall's Tavern), we were found by Dr. McGuire, who at once took charge of the wounded man. Through the night, back over the battle-field of the afternoon, we reached the Wilderness store, and in a field on the north the field-hospital of our corps under Dr. Harvey Black. Here we found a tent prepared, and after midnight the left arm was amputated near the shoulder, and a ball taken from the right hand.

All night long it was mine to watch by the sufferer, and keep him warmly wrapped and undisturbed in his sleep. At nine a.m., on the next day, when he aroused, cannon firing again filled the air, and all the Sunday through the fierce battle raged, General J.E.B. Stuart commanding the Confederates in Jackson's place. A dispatch was sent to the commanding general to announce formally his disability, – tidings General Lee had received during the night with profound grief. There came back the following note:

General: I have just received your note, informing me that you were wounded. I cannot express my regret at the occurrence. Could I have directed events, I should have chosen, for the good, of the country, to have been disabled in your stead.

I congratulate you upon the victory which

is due to your skill and energy.
                    Most truly yours,
                        R.E. Lee, *General.*

When this dispatch was handed to me at the tent, and I read it aloud, General Jackson turned his face away and said, "General Lee is very kind, but he should give the praise to God."

The long day was passed with bright hopes for the wounded general, with tidings of success on the battle-field, with sad news of losses, and messages to and from other wounded officers brought to the same infirmary.

On Monday, the general was carried in an ambulance, by way of Spotsylvania Court House, to most comfortable lodging at Chandler's, near Guinea's Station, on the Richmond, Fredericksburg, and Potomac railroad. And here, against our hopes, notwithstanding the skill and care of wise and watchful surgeons, watched day and night by wife and friends, amid the prayers and tears of all the Southern land, thinking not of himself, but of the cause he loved, and for the troops who had followed him so well and given him so great a name, our chief sank, day by day, with symptoms of pneumonia and some pains of pleurisy, until at 3:15 p.m., on the quiet of the Sabbath afternoon, May 10th, 1863, he raised himself from his bed, saying, "No, no, let us pass over the river, and rest under the shade of the trees"; and, falling again to his pillow, he passed away, "over the river," where, in a land where warfare is not known or feared, he rests forever "under the trees."

His shattered arm was buried in the family burying-ground of the Ellwood place – Major J. H. Lacy's – near his last battle-field.

His body rests, as he himself asked, "in Lexington, in the Valley of Virginia." The spot where he was so fatally wounded in the shades of the Wilderness is marked by a large quartz rock, placed there by the care of his chaplain and friend, the Rev. Dr. B.T. Lacy, and the latter's brother, Major J.H. Lacy, of Ellwood.

Others must tell the story of Confederate victory at Chancellorsville. It has been mine only, as in the movement of that time, so with my pen now, to follow my general himself. Great, the world believes him to have been in many elements of generalship; he was greatest and noblest in that he was good, and, without a selfish thought, gave his talent and his life to a cause that, as before the God he so devoutly served, he deemed right and just.

64864658R10087

Made in the USA
Charleston, SC
16 December 2016